THE

DHARMA
OF DOGS

our best friends as spiritual teachers

AN ANTHOLOGY EDITED BY
TAMI SIMON

sounds true
BOULDER, COLORADO

Sounds True
Boulder, CO 80306

Published 2017

Cover design by Jennifer Miles
Book design by Beth Skelley

Cover image © JPagetRFPhotos; shutterstock.com

"The Deeper Chance" by Mark Nepo (page 200) is reprinted from *The Way Under the Way* by Mark Nepo
(Boulder, CO: Sounds True, 2016).
"The Only Task" by Mark Nepo (page 202) is reprinted from *Things That Join the Sea and the Sky* by Mark Nepo
(Boulder, CO: Sounds True, 2017).

Printed in South Korea

Library of Congress Cataloging-in-Publication Data
Names: Simon, Tami, editor.
Title: The Dharma of dogs : our best friends as spiritual teachers / edited by Tami Simon.
Description: Boulder, CO : Sounds True, 2017.
Identifiers: LCCN 2016049625 (print) | LCCN 2017011429 (ebook) | ISBN 9781622037414 (pbk.) | ISBN 9781622037421 (ebook)
Subjects: LCSH: Dog owners—Psychology. | Dogs—Effect of human beings on—Anecdotes. |
    Dogs—Psychological aspects—Anecdotes. | Human-animal relationships—Anecdotes.
Classification: LCC SF422.86 .D44 2017 (print) | LCC SF422.86 (ebook) | DDC 636.7—dc23
LC record available at https://lccn.loc.gov/2016049625

10 9 8 7 6 5 4 3 2 1

Contents

ABOVE Jasmine

LEFT Raspberry and Tami

Introduction

Tami Simon

As a young person, I often felt like an alien who was somehow deposited on planet Earth. From the outside, people couldn't tell if I was a boy or a girl (or so they said), and on the inside, I wasn't even sure I was human. Humans seemed so coarse to me, and the world barbaric. I took refuge in ideas and literature and kept my sensitivity and heart locked away in a very secret place.

Many years later, after dropping out of college, traveling to Asia to study meditation, and starting a publishing company called Sounds True, I met Jasmine, a tall, blonde, floppy-eared cocker spaniel. I was thirty-nine years old. By that time, I had found meaningful work and a certain expansive quietness in the practice of meditation. I had also been in several intimate relationships that didn't quite take root. I knew how to meditate, work long hours, and talk about ideas. I didn't yet know how to feel connected and at home on Earth.

Jasmine became a heart teacher and healer for me (one of her nicknames was Dr. J). She wiggled her way right into the center of my heart, breaking through the outer protective shell, and she left accompanied by a huge heart-level combustion that forever changed me.

Jasmine came into my life along with Julie Kramer, who has been my partner in love for the past fifteen years and is now my wife. In many ways, my love with Jas (pronounced *Jazz*) paralleled and was deeply connected to my love with Julie. They both moved from British Columbia to Boulder to live with me just a few weeks after Julie and I met. Their arrival heralded a turning point.

1

Jas was three years old at the time, and not particularly well-behaved. However, she quickly sensed the new love configuration and seemed determined to win me over. And win me over she did. How did this "piglet with a halo" (another one of Jas's many nicknames) do it? How did she crack a shell nearly four decades strong?

It was the *constancy* of her love.

Jas followed me everywhere, and her heart-light was always switched to "on," maintaining a connection with me. I could feel her around even when we weren't together. To say she was devoted is an understatement. She followed me into every room. (It always amazed me that even when she seemed fast asleep, and even in her old age with total deafness and partial blindness, if I tiptoed out of the room, trying to not disturb her, she would immediately wake up and follow me.) Jas had extrasensory sensors, and they informed her how to fulfill what appeared to be her life mandate, which at all times was to "stay close and connected."

Although Jas came into my life as Julie's dog, she soon became our dog, and I started bringing her to work with me at Sounds True. We have a dog-friendly policy such that all well-behaved dogs (and cats and birds, for that matter) are allowed to join their human companions at work. On any given day, there might be one hundred employees at Sounds True along with fifteen to twenty canines, a feline, and occasionally a parakeet or two (obviously kept in separate offices).

Within no time, Jas started coming to work with me every day. From the time Jas was three to the time she was seventeen, she was by my side at Sounds True. At one point, I commented that she started to feel like "a third leg" because I always felt her with me.

Jas was a continual source of inner brightness for me. She didn't have to do anything or even not do anything to be such a source. All I had to do was look at her. How did this blonde, floppy-eared cocker spaniel have such an effect on me, even if she was just sleeping or looking out the window?

I think it was, quite simply, the power of her heart. The power of Jas's heart activated mine. Her constancy was a sun that melted my guard. Coming into relationship with her devoted dogginess made it safe for me to feel my humanness.

Jas lived to seventeen years of age. Toward the end of her life, she was on a host of Chinese herbs and received acupuncture once a week. I would have done anything to keep her alive longer, but at a certain point she developed a brain tumor and it was (more than) obvious that it was her time to leave. When we gave her the injection that would soon stop her heart, Julie, who is a shamanic practitioner, played her frame drum and whistled and sang with the most beatific look on her face, like she was accompanying Jas on some type of ecstatic journey. I, on the other hand, was crumpled over Jas's body wailing and sobbing. I was not spiritually detached. I was earthly attached to this beautiful body that had warmed the parts of me that were cold, that had befriended me in a way that no one else ever had.

Historically, detachment has been easy for me, to lean back and observe and know that everything is a flow of impermanence. But this was something different and new, and I gave myself totally to the experience. What I found was that the utter heartbreak that I felt around the loss of Jas opened a gateway in me—a red-hot, aching gateway—that showed me the kind of courage it takes to love with all my might, and to experience loss.

Fueling my spiritual search from a young age was a very simple human desire to feel connected, to feel like I belong to earthly existence. Jas, with her pure dog heart, was an emissary of the earth. You could say also that she was an emissary of the *dharma*, of the universal teachings about love and generosity and goodness. Through her devotion and friendship, she offered me a way home, a way to be here, instead of defended against the pain of being here. She gave me the gift of breaking my heart so I could land on my feet and offer and receive a full embrace.

A mentor of mine said, "The human heart is the only organ that grows stronger through being broken." Jas's death broke my heart, and in the best kind of way. It broke my heart open to loving mightily and losing and then wanting to love mightily again.

For some of us—for people like me—dogs carry a certain "medicine," a certain set of healing powers and properties that are unique to them and to their species. Loving and losing Jas and working in close proximity to a menagerie of dogs each day, it became apparent to me that "dog medicine"

3

has certain particular qualities that certain humans need and cherish. What is that medicine and how can we know it and describe it?

Another way to ask this question is, "What is the dharma of dogs?" In Indian philosophy, each one of us is said to possess a particular dharma, a particular purpose and work in the world that is unique to us and of benefit to others. Might there be a dharma of dogs—a particular way that dogs express their innate gifts and fulfill a certain purpose in relationship with human beings?

This is the question that we posed to thirty-one different writers and spiritual teachers in *The Dharma of Dogs*. From how to "just be," to teachings on naturalness, play, impermanence, joy, devotion, and loving and losing and loving again, we learned from the contributors how valuable—and life-changing—the relationship with a special dog can be. We have also included photos of the contributors and their canine companions because sometimes the essence of a friendship can best be communicated visually, by our facial expressions and how we are together, not just in words.

And by the way, I have a new dog in my life. Her name is Raspberry (although she most often goes by one of her nicknames: Raz (sounds a lot like Jas, huh?), Razzle Dazzle, the Dazzler, or most commonly Razcal. She is a one-year-old, black, curly-haired, mischievous, twenty-two-pound "spoodle"—half cocker spaniel, half poodle. I am still getting to know her and her particular dharma. For one thing, she is an extrovert (Julie and I both are not!), and she seems to revel in getting us to get off the couch and chase her (because she has a shoe or my reading glasses or a pen in her mouth) and take her to the dog park to play with other dogs (where I am asked to interact, oh my, with other humans and make small talk). Maybe she will teach me how to connect with others in a relaxed and easy way? That would be quite a teaching.

Finally, there is a certain specialness in *The Dharma of Dogs* being published by Sounds True, given our dog-friendly culture and all our furry friends in the building. It is a company so dog-friendly that one business consultant from New York City, when visiting our offices for the first time, wondered if we were running a kennel club as well as being a multi-media publishing company.

Sounds True's animal-friendly policy began back in the early 1990s. At the time, I was living with a blue heeler–Australian shepherd mix named Toby. I remember going to work each morning and leaving Toby at home and how sad Toby was as I gathered my bits and pieces preparing to leave. One morning, Toby cocked his head and looked at me with the saddest face in the world, and I just couldn't stand it. I brought him to Sounds True that day to share my office with me. It only took a few hours before several other people at Sounds True asked if they could bring their dogs to work as well. And that's how it started. Today we have an entire section of our employee handbook describing our dog-friendly policies (which includes a section on "three poops inside and you're out," although this is hard to strictly enforce).

In my opinion, the dogs at Sounds True keep us sane (and I am not exaggerating!). They ask us to pause from time to time, to stop pushing through and instead take a walk and breathe the outside air and take in the expansive sky. They remind us of the immediacy of a loving exchange that is always available, even with deadlines looming. They are guardians of the work of our heart, which is at the end of the day the true focus of our publishing mission—to open hearts to the immediacy of life. It is my great joy to be able to dedicate *The Dharma of Dogs* to all of the wondrous dogs of Sounds True—past, present, and still to come.

With a woof woof!

Tami Simon
January 2017
Boulder, Colorado

ABOVE Marlowe and Laura

The Gift of Poetry

Laura Pritchett

He came from a shelter in Minnesota during a winter when I was young and sad and he too was young and sad, and perhaps I just hoped we'd journey together sadly. I was suffering from Seasonal Affective Disorder, or perhaps just early-twenties confusion—and he was suffering from being someone's Christmas-puppy present left at the shelter once the holidays ended. We each had our problems.

I adopted him and changed his name from Zane to Marlowe after the poet Christopher Marlowe who loved nature; and perhaps after Raymond Chandler's fictional character Philip Marlowe, who had a lot of figuring out to do; or perhaps even after Marlow in Joseph Conrad's *Heart of Darkness* because he had his own brand of dark to struggle with. I am, after all, an author. That was my big dream back then—to write novels and short stories—though I had yet to publish a single thing. But I knew my literary references, and I knew they'd give me some hope. As would the dog.

Marlowe and I started walking. We walked in bone-biting Minnesota winters and in the humid summers. We moved and walked in Indiana, and then we moved again and walked in Colorado. I did the math once. We must have put on 14,000 miles together: three miles a day for perhaps 345 days a year for fourteen years. We could have walked across the country a couple of times; we could have hiked down to Peru. But all we ever did was explore our home; his black-tipped ears bounced up and down as he shuffled along.

It occurs to me now that Marlowe is gone—he's been gone a decade—that he changed me from a person who walked (between classes in college or for a stroll with a boyfriend) to a walk-*er*. As in, a person who every day needs a walk, and if a walk isn't had, well, something is amiss with the day, something is amiss with life.

It wasn't any kind of walking. It was contemplative, mindful, poetic walking.

What that dog helped me see—really see—was my home, my inner state of mind, my issues, and my stories. My internal and external landscape. At least, he taught me to *start* seeing (there are always more layers to uncover, after all). He taught me to pay attention. He gave me a truer love for the natural world.

In other words, I believe he taught me to walk with poetry. To be a poet. His literariness came through.

There was the deer he'd spot first.

The frog he'd stop and tilt his head at.

The rattlesnake he'd regard from afar.

His curiosity made me curious; his ability to stop and consider something slowed me up enough to make me do the same. Always, through his movement, he helped me understand this one spot on Earth where we had settled. Up some pine-scented trail he'd go, turn and look at me, ask me to notice, and then lead me on to my next destination.

He bore witness, too. He watched me through graduate school, through the birth of children, and through careers (he liked my writing career best, because it meant I was always home where he could sleep at my feet and demand walks at will). He helped me be silly; he helped me stay in shape. He cleaned off the kids' highchairs so that I didn't have to, and later he walked with them to the bus stop. He moved to several states and several homes within those states, but he also joined me on every conceivable type of trip. He sat on my lap as we drove across the entire state of Nebraska in 100-degree weather with the heater on in an attempt to cool the radiator. In Colorado, he chased a coyote and then sprinted behind *my legs* when the coyote started to chase *him*. He pulled me on cross-country skis. He swam with me in mountain lakes. He sat in canoes. He camped across Colorado. He almost died pinned against a grate in rushing water in a river.

He was also a *dog*. Marlowe imbued his dogness in a very pure way. Like all dogs, he had his quirks and preferences, which included romping with dead animals, rolling in manure, and running off, feigning deafness when something sparked his fancy. He understood my tone of voice when I admonished him for such things or tried to teach him otherwise, but he never apologized. He just looked up at me, pure dogness in his eyes, and there was nothing I could do except sigh and usually smile and give him a bath or leash him during the parts of the walk that were high-temptation areas.

Marlowe was fun to watch. From the back, he looked like Charlie Chaplin, shuffling along. From the side, he looked confusing—perhaps some collie, perhaps some Lab, perhaps some retriever? From the front, he looked like love, with those golden eyes and panting mouth and so-happy-to-be-alive disposition. He was so thoroughly dog that he made me want to be more thoroughly human.

More or less, he went through most of my adult life with me, from the unsure and uncentered twenties to the more solid and finding-myself thirties. And then he was done. Moving, that is. I walked out of my bedroom one morning and found him unable to rise off his bed. I stood over him and lifted his body so that he could put weight on his feet, and, like a strange-looking animal, we shuffled together outdoors. Sometimes he would find his footing, other times not. A few days of this and I knew: Marlowe was done walking.

What Marlowe really did was ask me to try to live life with poetry. Or at least, he set a very fine example.

I was okay; he was okay. It felt like a natural conclusion. I felt oddly at peace, oddly without suffering, because he had taught me that, too: what is—well, that's what *is*. Suffering comes from resisting. Looking back, I am struck by how little I grieved—and it was not because I didn't love him, for I did, but because his death seemed so natural, so full of grace. Or perhaps I did grieve, but it was in a settled, clear-hearted place. Perhaps he taught me to "use death as your advisor" because he lived well and he died well, without resistance but with wonder.

He's buried next to a pine tree in the Colorado foothills—near the sage and sunflowers and mountain mahogany—the landscape he had lived in the longest, the one he'd protected (mainly from what I'm sure he considered ferocious deer, although he did actually chase away a bear). The kids dropped love notes, a ball, a bone, a blanket, a stuffed animal into his grave. I frequently walk by his burial place with a new dog, whom I love as well, and I nod at Marlowe.

I noticed a few years ago that every single one of my novels—I did become a published writer—has a large, oddball dog in it. In my fictional world, I have named them Satchmo, Ringo, Dog, Ruby—I can't remember them all, there have been so many dogs—but each is some manifestation of Marlowe. So in the end, he went back from whence he came—from books and into books, where the dog is always a bit of a hero.

What Marlowe really did was ask me to try to live *life* with poetry. Or at least, he set a very fine example. I'd like to think that each day I see something anew, through his eyes, even now that he's gone. I may not have his constant guidance in these matters, but some of his lessons linger and are ingrained. Perhaps I am more apt to notice the muskrat sliding into the water, the way the trail splits, the joy of a good smell. I stop to consider the slant of sunlight on mountain mahogany seeds; the fawn and I consider each other carefully. Surely I've got some distance to go in this regard, but there's no doubt that there's an absolute awareness in which I experience my days, experience my walks, am curious about the odd and lovely details of the natural world. At such times, I thank him for helping me walk—with some poetry, I hope—through my life.

ABOVE Tashi and Andrew

My Little Buddha

Andrew Holecek

In the magical world of Tibetan Buddhism, it is said that the *tulkus,* or "awakened ones," are able to take rebirth in any form, including that of an animal. They do so as a way to benefit others. I have no idea if this is true; however, I do know that I am in need of benefit, and that there is much that my dog Tashi has taught me. I often look at Tashi as my little Buddha, and I do my best to stay open to his teachings.

Seeing and Being the Divine

Tashi, a fourteen-pound ball of cotton (hence the French breed name Coton de Tulear), has delivered many silent sermons over the years. I realize that I am anthropomorphizing—or in this case deifying—his behavior and projecting my own lesson plan upon his actions, but I'll take a teaching wherever I can get it, even if it's one that I project.

The main lesson Tashi conveys, as many pet owners can attest to, is that of unconditional love. He doesn't just love *me* unconditionally, he loves *everybody*. Tashi greets my sweet neighbor Bill, whom I like, the same way he greets my grumpy neighbor Fred, whom I can't stand. That's real equanimity. I can't do what Tashi does. It doesn't matter who we bump into on our walks; what I perceive as good, bad, or ugly, he perceives as a long-lost friend. I aspire to attain his balanced approach toward everyone.

Tashi greets me with wild enthusiasm every time I come home. If I'm feeling good, bad, or ugly, it doesn't matter to him. I don't greet (or treat) myself with the same zeal and equanimity that he greets me. Tashi always lifts me up and helps me remember the maxim, "May I be the person that my dog thinks I am."

Tashi takes this maxim a notch higher. In my study of Buddhism, I work with the practice of pure perception, which is about seeing the world and the beings that inhabit it as sacred. It's a potent "fake it until you make it" practice. Pure perception is about not getting caught up in profane superficial appearances but seeing through that veneer into the innate purity that lies below. With his unconditional love toward me, Tashi reminds me of this celestial-view teaching: "May I be the divine being that the Buddhas know I am. May I see through the profanity of mere appearance and into the sacred truth within."

Play of the Universe

I'm a complex guy with a convoluted mind, someone who tends to get lost in a disembodied headspace. I'm working on it, but I'm afraid I'm still a fusty intellectual. Tashi punctures this inflated complexity and brings me back to earth. His simplicity is disarming, a kind of mind-eraser for me. He shows me that complexity doesn't stand a chance against simplicity. When he darts around in sheer delight with his stuffed "piggy" squeaking in his mouth, I can't help but drop all my snooty thoughts, fall into the preciousness of the present moment, and squeal with my own delight as I run after him and into his pure, embodied world. My furrowed brow is replaced with an impish grin as he liberates me from my self-importance.

Tashi takes it further—delivering another significant lesson. He reminds me, as both the Hindus and Buddhists assert, that the absolute nature of reality is one of play (*lila* in Hinduism; *rolpa* in Tibetan Buddhism). Play is activity done without purpose—for the sheer heck of it—and is always defined by a sense of embodied presence. When I am being playful, especially with my dog, I discover that I'm not thinking about the past or worrying about the future. I'm fully participating in life, bolted into the present moment, free of all concepts. When I reflect (and none of this reflection happens when I'm actually playing, of course, which would defeat the spirit of play; it happens when my silly mind steps in later), I'm temporarily plugged into something primal, a faint echo of the play that is this very cosmos.

Tashi is also a rivet into reality when he brings me back to my senses. His world is a highly sensual one, and our senses only operate in the present. I can't smell the future or see the past; I can't taste the future or hear the past. My senses are forever

I aspire to attain his balanced approach toward everyone.

nailed into the present moment, which is where life happens and which is where my time with Tashi takes me. *He* holds the leash when I follow his lead into the fully embodied present moment, which is where he always walks.

Shakes and Barks

I have a very sticky mind, like Velcro. I glom onto things, mostly negative, and tend to catastrophize even the smallest events. It's embarrassing how I keep situations alive long after they should be dead. Tashi continually teaches me how to let go. Whenever he gets hurt, like when I inadvertently step on his paw, there may be a brief yelp. But he tosses it off, the same way that he shakes off water when he steps out of a pond. He doesn't spin the momentary insult into a drama or hold a grudge. I occasionally mimic this physical gesture when something really gummy is getting me down. I'll physically "throw it off," like Tashi does the water on his back, and often feel lighter because of the "Tashi toss."

Like any pup, Tashi has his quirks. One in particular is very revealing. When it gets dark, he barks at the slightest hint of someone or something outside. If I take him for a walk at night, he often barks at trash cans and various shadowy forms. He projects a dangerous entity that is not there. It's so sweet, because he's just trying to protect me. Or maybe that's *my* projection? From my perspective it's endearing and often hilarious, but from his perspective it's deadly serious. His fear is real, even though the objects that trigger it are not. When I'm in the house at night, he'll often bark at absolutely nothing outside. I used to check the door to see if somebody was indeed there, but it was always nothing. He's afraid of something nonexistent. Out of fear, he's defending me from nothing.

Here's the dharma behind this, and it is weighty. At the heart of Buddhism lie the profound teachings on emptiness, which proclaim that if you look closely at anything, you will find no inherent "thingness." This is because things are empty of inherent existence. Emptiness doesn't mean nothingness (which would be nihilistic); it means no-*thing*ness. It means there's a big difference between appearance (the way things seem to be) and reality (the way things truly are). The path is about bringing appearance into harmony with reality. Human beings suffer because we take things to be truly existent, exactly the same way we suffer from a nightmare when we take the contents of the bad dream to be real. The Buddha ("awakened one") woke up from the façade of mere appearance and into the truth of reality. He woke up from the nightmare of imputed existence.

When it comes to Tashi's fear of what he sees in the dark—the way he projects threatening entities where there are none, and the way he barks at absolutely nothing out there—he drives home an important lesson on emptiness. When I mistake things "out there" to be real (which gives birth to duality), imputing existence and potential danger upon illusory entities that arise out of the darkness of my ignorance, I realize I'm not so different from my dog. Hinduism's Upanishads proclaim, "Where there is other, there is fear." So, when I bark at the mere appearance of others out of my fear that there's something really out there, I realize my bond with Tashi. We share the same primal fear.

There are important differences, and the depth of this lesson continues. In order for Tashi to evolve out of the animal realm, he *needs* his fear. In order for me to evolve out of the human realm, I need to *transcend* mine. Otherwise I will continue to howl at things that aren't there and defend an illusory entity (ego) that's actually hurting me. In order for me to go from ego (the archetypal "thing") to egoless ("thinglessness") or from beast to Buddha, I need to evolve past the very fear that got me to this evolutionary point.

This is one reason that spiritual evolution is tricky and that this lesson from Tashi is so deep. The fear I need to transcend is hardwired into my system. To evolve, I need to understand what got me here physically (healthy fear), and what now keeps me from getting there spiritually (an improper relationship to that fear). It's an integral approach to fear, which means honoring and incorporating its facilitating biological role while simultaneously transcending its spiritual limitations. Fear has its place. We need to locate that place and keep it there. Tashi's fear of something that doesn't exist drives home this critical point.

Dog's Gaze

One of my favorite things to do is have Tashi chase stuff. I especially like "fooling" him with my laser pointer. He loves to run after the red dot on my white carpet, certain that the next time he pounces he'll finally get what he's after. This activity always reminds me of one of the great teachings in Dzogchen, considered the highest school in Tibetan Buddhism, called "The Lion's Gaze."

This teaching says that if you throw a stick out and away from a dog, the dog will chase after the stick. I can confirm that. However, if you throw a stick out and away from a lion, the lion will chase after *you*. Even though I've been to Africa and seen many lions, I've never tried to confirm this. I still respect the fear that keeps me physically alive!

According to Dzogchen, we all have the gaze of the dog. It's only the sticks that are different. Look closely at your mind. We are forever chasing the sticks thrown out by our own minds, running endlessly after the thoughts and emotions tossed within. A thought pops up and we dash after it. An emotion comes up and we get swept away with it. That outward gaze and subsequent movement points us in the wrong direction. By running after thoughts, the "gaze of the dog" is forever seduced into the world of sticks, sucked into the realm of form. As the song says, "We're looking for love [*and everything else we want*] in all the wrong places." We're looking outside of ourselves for happiness.

As with thoughts, so with things. As inside, so outside. It's not just mental forms that we chase, but physical ones. I'm just like Tashi. But instead of chasing sticks I run after stocks, or spicy experiences, or ideologies. Sticks come in many sizes and shapes. It doesn't matter if it's a thought, an emotion, a car, house, lover, or a job. Most of us are infatuated with form, subtle or gross, and run after it. In so doing we ensure our suffering, because everything composed of form will eventually decay and die. Sticks ultimately rot.

The teaching, of course, is that we'll never find lasting happiness outside. Sorry, Tashi! When he pulls on his leash, yanking to get to a spot on the grass that seems just like the spot he is on, I'll often say, "Happiness doesn't exist over there, bud. No matter how hard you tug, you're not going to get what you want over there."

Unconditional happiness can only be found within. Meditation and contemplation swap the dog's gaze with the lion's gaze and point us in the right direction. Instead of chasing after a thought and losing yourself in the world of form, follow the thought back to its source and *find* your true Self in the world of formlessness. Follow the stick back to its thrower, and you will discover what you're really looking for.

This is such a central teaching in Buddhism that even the Tibetan words for "Buddhist" (*nangpa*) and "non-Buddhist" (*chipa*) allude to it. *Nangpa* means "insider" and *chipa* means "outsider." Buddhists are those who realize that happiness is an inside job. Tashi's pursuit of external happiness reminds me of this truth.

Is my Tashi a tulku? Why not? He certainly delivers the teachings befitting a fluffy Buddha. The dog costume fools me now and again, but thick as I am, I'm starting to get it.

ABOVE Charlie and Alice

I Had No Idea
Charlie Was Coming

Alice Walker

One day my former partner, a musician, said he'd met an interesting woman at a party and he was sure she and I would like each other. He was at the party looking for a drummer, I believe, to play with his quintet. I said sure, invite her over. She came. With her came the smallest, cutest dog I had ever seen: a tiny Yorkie, whose name was Charlie. I liked the woman well enough—she lived on an island in Greece and raised oregano and lavender, so as a gardener and traveler I found her interesting—but the dog enchanted me. He followed her everywhere, like a separate little part of her, and when she sat down, he let her know, by gently plucking at her skirt, he'd like to be picked up. As they drove away, his soulful brown eyes stayed with me.

Actually, I think I said to her: If you ever need a home for your dog, think of me. But I never thought anything would come of it. Weeks went by. We heard more of the drama of Charlie's young life: he'd been abandoned as a puppy because—and here I am guessing—his humans didn't know how to care for him. As I've said, Charlie is a Yorkie, or Yorkshire terrier, six and a half pounds, and a lot of him is hair. The hair of Yorkies seems to grow while you're looking at it. Anyway, when he was found (as he was about to encounter an open drain in the middle of the street), he was entangled in his own hair. He was rescued by my new friend's daughter and her young daughters, and he had lived happily with them for a couple of years. Now that family was in disarray: divorce, moving, new lives for everyone in the offing, and so Grandmother, with whom I'd met Charlie, had temporarily inherited him. She clearly adored him, but a life with him among the lavender and oregano fields in Greece seemed a stretch for her.

So, less than a month after our meeting, Charlie, along with his entire human family, arrived at my door. Grandmother, mother, daughter, granddaughters. They were some of the saddest looking humans I'd seen in my life. They'd brought his favorite little sweater (in which he still sleeps on chilly nights), his brushes and combs, some food, and also an unscented, brand-new toy wrapped in plastic so that no scent of them would remain to further intensify his homesickness—which they were right to anticipate. For he was dreadfully sad when they left! He whimpered and cried and tried to rush after them. My heart broke to feel his distress. And of course he could not bear to be consoled by my partner or me.

And then my partner and I thought of something.

We decided to take Charlie on a long walk on what we call the Upper Trail. It is just a logging road that was used years ago when the hills I live in were covered with old-growth redwood forests that have long since been cut down. It winds through the forest past giant rocks and returning trees, and a few (in season) rushing waterfalls.

Charlie began to tire, visibly, as we made our way to the end of this trail; by the time we started back, his tongue was hanging out. That is when I scooped him up in my arms and cuddled him close to my heart. I carried him all the way back to the house; by the time we reached home, he had listened to the steadiness of my heartbeat long enough to know he could trust me. And that maybe, with my partner and me, he had found a second home.

We don't know how old he is, but Charlie has been with us for almost four years. It seems he has been a part of us forever. And even though we no longer share a home, both of us continue to share an abiding love for Charlie.

What does he give us? Unconditional love, uninhibited delight whenever we've been away and he once again (glory be!) sees us. I used to love to watch him when we were expecting his "daddee" and the sound of his motorcycle began to hum on the air. I used to joke that Charlie could hear the motorcycle when it was started up in Berkeley, almost three hours away. Or, when I was away and flying home again after a sometimes arduous, if not perilous, journey, Charlie would somehow know and begin to sit by the front window waiting for me to appear at the gate.

There is a welcome, a joy, a delirium of delight that dogs offer us that makes it impossible for us to believe we are not loved. And to know that love is a good thing to share whatever the form! Charlie's entire body speaks the language of acceptance, engagement, and pleasure at my presence. It's true this is doubled if I'm carrying food, but even without it, I am reminded that no matter what dreadful news is coming over the airwaves about the coldness and despair of our human situation, love is a constant in this world. No being exhibits this quality better than Charlie, and all the other dogs without whose irrepressible teaching humans would perhaps forget.

It is taught that the Buddha had many lifetimes as various animals before he took human form. He was probably a dog just before becoming a Buddha.

There is a welcome, a joy, a delirium of delight that dogs offer us that makes it impossible for us to believe we are not loved.

ABOVE Whippet (center), Jeri, and Sadie (left)

Lost Dog

Jeri Parker

She's weak on her legs now," the guy who saw her last told me.

My own legs felt shaky and I pictured her—those earnest brown eyes, just this side of beseeching; that silly coat, not quite finished, a scant tufting of white and then those long whispets of hair over the undercoat. You almost couldn't call it fur. She was barely covered, and I knew it wouldn't be enough to keep her warm out there in the forest. And the tall legs, slightly out of phase with the rest of her—and she was weak on them now.

Everyone in my little mountain community knew Whippet was lost, and everyone asked for a description. But one woman said, "What is she like?"

"Hapless," I answered. "Not quite timid. Just the dog you should never let get confused, get lost." That was the first time I cried. I'd let both of those things occur. I'd opened the back door and watched her go out early for her run. I hadn't thought anything about having loaned my car to my friend Pauline, hadn't imagined that Whippet might come back to the cabin, see the car gone, and race back down the trail, looking for me in the three million acres of Targhee National Forest that stretch through southeastern Idaho and into Montana and Wyoming.

I glanced at my watch. Time was going to be important, was going to be crucial. I had already let an hour go by, maybe more. I'd had a warning, but I didn't see it as that. My cat, Michael, had come in earlier. I try to reconstruct it—it could have been two hours earlier. He was alone. Why hadn't I noticed that? He never came in without Whippet. Then he stood in the middle of the dining room and bawled.

I'd never heard him do that either, or any cat, for that matter. There was urgency and anxiety in every sound he made, every move he made, and I'd laughed at him and gone back to my painting.

Whippet had been a gift of apology, so she came already charged with meaning. I called her Lapin La Chienne at first because she looked more rabbit than dog—a white bunny with searching, timid eyes. Maybe not so much timid as pleading not to be made timid. She rode on my shoulder in the car when she was little, and she still tried to get up there to watch the road. She slept against my back.

She didn't like me to paint, although she had very few dislikes. She must have felt how unavailable I was when I got out the brushes, the tubes of color, the canvas. That's what I'd done that morning—and not just painting, but painting in her room, my supplies spread across the bed she slept on during the day.

It seemed like ten minutes, but it was probably more like an hour and a half before Michael had come in and begun to bawl and I'd kept on painting. I don't know what finally made me look up and realize something was wrong. I stepped out on the porch. "Whippet," I called. I tried to calculate the time she'd gone out. I ran to the driveway. "Driveway" is too big a word—it was barely a path through the trees. When she didn't come—when had she *ever* not come?—I ran to the bottom of the hill, calling. And that's when I understood what it meant to not have a car. I pictured her out there in the forest, those tall white legs of hers against black tree trunks, and my heart skipped around. She'd be highly visible; that was reassuring. You'd be able to see her for miles up there on those high, thin legs of hers.

She wasn't actually a whippet. One look at her told you her pedigree was a scramble. I always thought a goat was in there somewhere, and actually that word came up in the search. She had that flimsy coat—it was like she'd run out one coat and then changed her mind and run out a half-finished overcoat. Her eyebrows flopped. I should have named her The Whispet.

You keep yourself from panic as long as you can when you're the responsible party. Then suddenly it has you. I ran to Pat's, my nearest neighbor. It was about a four-minute walk, a one-minute run.

"Whippet's gone!" I said.

"She'll be back," Pat said in that don't-worry voice.

"She never doesn't come when I call," I said.

"She's out hunting," Pat assured me. "If she's not back in a few hours, I'll drive you around."

Those hours were spent walking through the forest calling, running, then stumbling and falling; you run so haphazardly, alarmed at your own voice. And all the while rehearsing her—how she fluffed a pillow for ten minutes before she sank into it, how she meticulously picked all the kibbles out of the Kibbles 'n Bits.

I try to calm myself and go back to my painting, a painting I will never finish. And then I'm off again, dropping the brush, running through the forest calling. There is real fear in my voice. The grasses of September brush against my legs. The scent of rabbitbrush and sage rise up. I see moose scat. I think of what's out there—those moose and elk and coyotes and wolves and porcupines and bear. I know about the bear. I had one come into the cabin and hang around with me one morning as though he were there for tea.

Dogs, I think. I wonder when they appeared. They would have roamed these mountains in wild packs thousands of years ago.

I had brought Whippet here to my cabin from the city and a fenced back yard. I'd introduced her to wildness, to danger. And bliss. But I'd failed to keep her from harm's way. My sense of responsibility for her safety, for her life, falls over me like a second skin. I fly back to my feet and I run hard now, calling, creating a grid in my mind. I work the upper acres and then drop down.

I'm expecting her to pop up every minute. I'm startled that she doesn't come, and I scan near, far out, and suddenly I'm inside-out with fear.

"I'll find you," I murmur as the trees go by. "I'll find you, Whippet," and I know I'll never stop looking. I see in my mind what a wolf can do to a dog, and I run back to Pat's. "Could I borrow your truck?" I ask, flat out, a note of desperation in my voice.

"Come on," she says, "let's drive around and look for her. I know we'll see her right off."

This wispy dog is my access to calm, and I try to get back to that calm as we drive along Stamp Meadows Road, the old logging route. I call her spirit to me, see myself up on the high bed with her, and I'm calling and calling and she doesn't come. I think of the joy in her and I miss it. I have those two things about me all the time when I'm with her—the calmness of Whippet and the joy in her. I know suddenly how long it will be before my own heart leaps up in joy if she stays out there in the forest—part of the food chain herself now, unequipped since I'd taken away her independence. I'd made her subservient to my judgment. I hadn't ever thought that that's what we're doing with our household pets.

That's when the bargaining starts. Great Spirit, let me have her back, I murmur. I'll understand my part in it—let me have her again. And I see her coming back, tired, relieved, and me lifting her to the bed. And she curls along my back, and I'm able to sleep.

I stretch out on the bed for a minute when I get back to the cabin. I wake hours later with a start. It's dark and I'm crying, and then I'm back to walking the pitch-black forest, calling out, "Whippet, I'm sorry. Whippet, come home."

I phone my friend Cill the next morning. "Can you come up early?" I ask. My voice catches. She's a nurse; she can't just walk off the job. But she does manage it; she'll be up right away, she tells me. I go outside and do my Indian prayer—arms outstretched. I feel in a different way what I have to be grateful for.

It's a five-hour drive for Cill. I walk in the forest the whole five hours. I think Whippet is close—just mixed up. When I come back to the cabin, Cill's big Plymouth van is in the driveway. Okay, we say, let's make a plan. We get out a map. I pencil in where I've been. We drive for hours, putting up rudimentary posters I'd made. Pat agrees to be the command post—she's the one with a phone.

The calls start coming in at once: She's been to the church. She's been to the huckleberry patch. She's been to the river. That's when the loggers tell me she's weak on her legs. They gave her a peanut butter sandwich, but she wouldn't eat it.

Stamp Meadows Road is a dustbowl now. The trucks and fishermen have gone up and down it all summer, and they've left about five inches of powder on it. We go back out there, over and over, and stop whenever we see anyone. "She chased a white one-ton," one of the sawyers tells me. Cill's truck is white and Whippet is well acquainted with it. My throat catches. I feel lightheaded.

We look until the dark obliterates everything. We go into Island Park Lodge for a late dinner. The waitress tells me she'd lost her husband, and then she'd lost her dog, and there was no difference in the emptiness. This bridge between us comforts me profoundly.

The third day is indistinguishable from the second. On the fourth day, a kind of peace falls over me. Whippet isn't hating every minute, I say to myself. She's stopping by the creek, lying down, feeling the cool breeze stir her fur. She looks up at Sawtell Peak at sunset. If she dies out there, Sawtell is a tombstone to make the pharaohs jealous. I relax.

"We'll have to be careful not to make her a folk dog when we find her," I tell Cill in the morning. And I go on, thinking aloud. "There's a certain comfort in knowing she isn't doing

They'd all offered unconditional love, trained me in what it was to have their companionship, and gave me access to how they understood day, night, summer, winter—nature itself. As well as the human heart.

to herself what we're doing—she isn't going through the reasoning why. Maybe we shouldn't be trying to second-guess her. There doesn't seem to be any pattern." I think that over. "Unless, you know, it looks like she's gone to all the places I took her." Why didn't I see that?

Day One: Bart sees her on that first little dip in the road leading away from the mill and back to the highway. Next sighting: She's continuing on that road; she's traveled two or three miles. Next sighting: It's Friday; she's on the logging roads at 9:00 and 11:30 a.m. And that's where she is at 6:00 p.m. when the loggers offered her a peanut butter sandwich. That area accounts for the second, third, fourth, fifth, and sixth sightings.

We'd been back to that spot fifty times. The guys who were stripping out lodgepoles in there know us by name now. That's where we got the "weak on her legs" report. She was farther up the road at 6:15 that third evening. Then she was back closer to the mill when Bart saw her at 3:30 p.m. on Friday, the beginning of the wild and furious Labor Day weekend. Then she was over by Island

Park Lodge Saturday evening and again Sunday morning at 8:00, 8:30, and 10:00. Then she went to Lee Swaner's cabin on the North Fork—we walked in there all the time. That same day she went up the hill—she'd have to be crossing the highway constantly—and she went to Janet's cabin. I'd taken her there the week before.

Cill says, "And Sunday she went to church."

"That's right," I laugh. She was at the church on Sunday. Had I taken her there? And then we didn't hear anything for a while.

I can't let myself think how often Whippet darted across that highway with its restless tourists driving too fast.

"This is the story of a lost dog," I say to Cill. "It goes like most lost dog stories. They saw her, but we didn't. Then they saw her again, but we didn't. Then no one saw her for quite a while, and we thought she was gone. Then they saw her again, but we didn't."

This went on for five days—not a very long time really, but it involves 120 hours—each with more minutes, it seemed, than the one before. Half of them are unlit by daylight—simple physics, but hard on the heart. It extended to twenty-two sightings—the most interesting of which went like this: "Where were you yesterday, Parker? I tried to call you for three hours. Your dog went over to that sign you put up at the church and laid down under it just like she could read." Whippet was the only dog I ever had who could have learned to read.

I'd had dogs from the time I was born. I always think of myself as a serious dog lover, not a slacker, but I've crossed over this time. I sit out on the deck in the sun and think of my dogs: Mike, the springer spaniel I had as a little girl. Ginger, our beautiful golden Chesapeake—there's a dog who got lost too. Blackie, the dog my father abandoned on a country road, the hardest to remember. Tami, the dog I drove to Montreal, packed in ice to keep cool. Mouse, who ate the shoes of my boyfriends when I had them distracted. Sadie, the little beagle, the delight of my first days in Utah. And then Whippet. They'd all offered unconditional love, trained me in what it was to have their companionship, and gave me access to how they understood day, night, summer, winter—nature itself. As well as the human heart.

"Let's go fishing," I say to Cill on the last day. We go to Coffee Pot. I've finally got so I'm not scanning every square inch of forest. We stand in the cool water and cast our lines, and a little sense of normalcy returns. It's such a beautiful world. When we get back to the cabin, I tell Cill I'm through looking. If someone called and said they had her right now, I wouldn't go after her.

The phone rang. "We've got her. She's at Island Park Lodge."

We grab the car keys. We don't take jackets or purses or anything. We know how fast this dog moves. When we get there I run into the lodge. "My dog . . . ?"

"She's right up there on that hill, hon," the waitress says. She's seen us in here often for breakfast. She's the one who told me, "I lost my husband, and then I lost my dog, and it was the same emptiness."

I run out to tell Cill, and I see her up on the hill. She's kneeling, and that crazy white dog—the white Whippet—is in her arms. I run as though she might disappear again, and then I have her bony little body in my arms, and I put my face down in that dusty fur and think of the trees and the river and the roads and the gentle people, and I love having this little shaman, this dog.

ABOVE Kusung and Lama Tsomo

Lama Kusung

Lama Tsomo

When Kusung (pronounced "koo-soong") arrived she was in grief and shock. Fair enough: at eight weeks of age, after her brothers and sisters had all been sold, she was sent away from home. During her first two weeks with me, she made tiny, high-pitched squeaks at the rate of about one per minute. She wandered around aimlessly, probably hoping in the next loop she would come upon her lost family. Those squeaks were the sound of her little heart breaking.

I have a master's degree in counseling psychology, so I have some idea of what we humans might do with such a traumatic experience. I bet you do, too. Many of us would find a way to dull the pain. We might resent our new "mom" and act out—anger and emotional blunting being two favorite human reactions.

Fortunately, Kusung knew better. Neither route would lead to satisfying love and happiness, and neither would bring joy into the world for herself or others. Quite the contrary. Oh, if only she could give advice to us humans. Think of the workshops and speaking tours she could do! Instead, she *demonstrated* a better route. I was the lucky audience.

I watched her simply suffer and express her suffering. At first she took some comfort in my lap, though she certainly knew it was a mere substitute—the only one at hand—for her family. But gradually she settled. She stopped her aimless rounds, and the squeaking slowed to almost nil. Soongma, her new "sister," was thrilled to have a canine playmate and determined to tempt Kusung to play. Soongma jumped back and forth, wagging furiously. She rolled belly-up, making the most alluring play-growls. Kusung was helpless before it all, and dove in.

Gradually she fell in love with me as her new "mom." *Really* fell in love. She *had* to be as close to me as possible, sleeping at my feet as I sat at my computer. Then moving camp to the bathroom for the minutes I was there. Then to the kitchen as I warmed up lunch. It went on until it was time for her to fall asleep in her crate, tucked up against my bed so that she could kiss my fingers goodnight from inside it.

When I talked to her, she would cock her head this way and that, seemingly determined to learn English as quickly as possible. Despite not having mastered the language, she found my silly, sweet-nothing talk riveting.

When we went outside for her thousand daily bathroom breaks, Kusung constantly rushed back and forth between her beloved sister and me, eager to play all day if we were game. We weren't. Fortunately, she did need a lot of beauty sleep. (And as you can see from our photograph, the sleep worked.)

The most beautiful thing about Kusung isn't her lush fur or her gorgeous face and bright eyes. It's definitely not her raw courage; although her name means "bodyguard" in Tibetan, she flees from new people. It's her loving heart. I've had and known a lot of dogs, and they all live for love. While we humans also live for love, we get distracted and confused about that main point.

So let me tell you, because Kusung won't bother: *it really is all about love.*

In almost any movie, book, or song, whether it's spelled out or not, love is the bottom line, but our fancy frontal lobes seem to cover that with undue complication. When something breaks our human hearts, we tend to go numb, wallow in self-pity, or indulge in righteous wrath. We distract and justify with our fancy human words and concepts, which flow in a never-ending stream.

Dogs don't do any of that. They're very clear that they're all about love, and they feel it and express it fully whenever they get the chance. They forgive because they don't see the fun in holding a grudge. They love again, even if their hearts have been broken. If they make a mistake and we scold them, they don't justify or blame-push. They're simply crestfallen, telling us, "I'm sorry!" with their whole bodies until we smile at them again. Relationship can be so simple. Really.

Kusung is now three years old. She still has to move camp to the kitchen when I heat up lunch, and to the bathroom when I go there. She loves to hold hands . . . for a long time. When I climb into bed at night, she jumps up and plops her rear end on my shoulder, her eighty-five-pound body along my arm, and proceeds to kiss my hand at the other end. Literally nose to tail, full contact. Most dogs want to be close by, but they still like a little bit of space. Not Kusung. She'd rest her wet nose right on my pillow if I let her.

Last year, when she was a wild, goofy teenager, I came down with the longest, most terrible bout of flu I've ever experienced. I was mostly bedridden for three months. You might be thinking the poor girl would have gone stir crazy, because she usually becomes antsy if she is inside and awake for more than a couple of hours. But I was out of commission for days, for weeks. And of course I was in no condition to entertain her.

It really is all about love.

If you've never been sick for a long time, you might not realize how isolating it can be. I found out. I couldn't talk for long because I would cough, and conversation was too exhausting anyway. When I'm on solitary retreat, I relish the time alone. When I'm meditating all day during such retreats, it's a powerful, rich experience. During this long illness, though, I was too incapacitated to do practice sessions. Even reading was too much effort.

Kusung understood it all perfectly well. That rambunctious, playful girl spent motionless hours in her signature full-body cuddle position on my bed, or she snuggled up to the whole length of my legs on the couch. She was helping her mom in the best way she knew. And she had it right. I could soak up all that love without having to expend an ounce of energy, hour after hour, day after day. She wasn't looking for fun. She didn't whine to go out and play. She didn't resent giving me attention. She just loved me.

Love is her superpower. Lost love hasn't dimmed it; self-justification hasn't dimmed it; her capacity to give and receive love remains constant and limitless. In watching Kusung, I receive a long, deep lesson in simply loving—fully, open-heartedly, no matter what.

Isn't that what the great masters always teach us?

ABOVE Zephyr and JP

Blessings from Zephyr

JP Sears

Twelve years ago I fell face first into the tutelage of a Zen master named Zephyr. He showed up when I needed help finding my lost heart, my playfulness, humor, ability to cry, and curiosity for life. My master was such a compelling teacher that most of the time I had no idea he was teaching me anything, yet somehow he knew how to slide through the limitations of my mind, allowing his grace, wisdom, and compassion to permeate my heart and soul. While I'd love to tell you stories of my trials, tribulations, face licks, and cuddles with the great Zephyr, I'd probably be too biased to do him justice. Instead, I'll step back and let him tell you our story . . .

I Arrive

My name is Zephyr. I'm a divine aspect of oneness who enjoys rolling in decomposing rodents. I decided to incarnate into a dog's body for a few reasons. First, doG is God spelled forward, so my current incarnation is a great way for me to experience who I really am. Second, the universe smells absolutely fascinating through a dog's nostrils! And third, there was a redheaded human who lost his heart and desperately needed help finding it. That human is JP, my dad. I'm not JP's biological son, but I've never told him that—I don't think he could handle it.

My dad's spiritual quest started when I—in glowing, freshly reincarnated Dalai Lama–like fashion—arrived in his life as an eight-week-old, three-pound maniac dachshund puppy. JP was 161 years old (twenty-three in human years, if that's how you count), had just moved to California, and was trying to make something of himself. He was struggling to make a living, terrible at playing fetch, insecure, and too scared to feel as scared as he really was. His heart was so calcified that he didn't even know he wanted me. Luckily for him, someone gave me to him as a gift, so he ultimately had to receive what he needed, even though he didn't want to at the time.

Tao of Being Grounded

As a teacher, I knew I had my work cut out for me right away. My dad was incredibly ungrounded in his emotions, as he lived in his head. (The lineage I come from recognizes that a *high* Intelligence Quotient is just code for a *low* Emotional Quotient.) His ability to rationalize anything caused him to outsmart himself, yet he was blind to the consequences—becoming increasingly disconnected from his emotional heart.

I commenced my dad's training. I began teaching from *The Doctrine of Puppy Teeth Piercing Skin*. I'd bite Dad's feet whenever he walked around the apartment without shoes on. I found his annoyance so amusing! He'd say, "Zephyr is just an obnoxious puppy giving my feet puncture wounds!" What he didn't realize was that I was getting his attention in the only way I could and teaching him to be grounded. He was so resistant to receiving this lesson that sometimes he would walk over the couch and hop onto a chair to get to the other end of the room, an external manifestation of how he strategizes to avoid his heart on the inside.

I put in two years of consistent foot-biting effort before Dad finally began to have the courage to keep his feet (and emotions) grounded. He is starting to learn how to fetch his own heart, at least a little bit, which is a lot better than when I began mentoring him.

Tao of Presence

Growing up in San Diego, I let my dad take me to the beach all the time. All I wanted to do when I was there was dig in the sand. My dad just loved to watch me dig. He often asked, "What are you digging for?" I would answer, not with words because he never learned to speak dog, but with the interpretive dance of more passionate digging that clearly said, "*What* am I digging for? To dig! There's no agenda. The joy of digging is always in the dig, not in what you find." I also ate a lot of sand. This wasn't for any particular teaching purpose; I just liked my dad's perplexed face as he wondered why I ate so much sand.

> Know that the world is overwhelmingly filled with love, except for vacuum cleaners—those are inherently evil.

Dad always looked to the future. His thoughts of what he was supposed to find blinded him to the pure bliss of having his nose in the sand of life and enjoying the dig for digging's sake. I'd let him believe he was enthralled with watching me dig, while in reality I knew he was beginning to feel the desire and delight of being present in his own journey instead of being so destination driven. Sometimes I would even rub myself in dead fish to congratulate him on how well he was practicing presence, but he has never known how to take a compliment.

Tao of Innocence

As time went on, my dad didn't need me to bite his feet as often. That made it easier for me to become the rawhide of his eye. He thought there was something about me that he just loved. The truth is that I did just the right amount of cute dog stuff to draw something important out of the underground well of my dad's unconscious. You see, long ago, before he can even remember, Dad turned his back on the pure innocence of his child self. I would never wish this on anyone, not even a pretentious cat. Dad unfortunately betrayed his own childlike gifts. There were times in his human puppyhood that he felt safer when he pretended to be in control, strong, and stable, instead of rooted in his authentic self. He buried it under the dirt of his façade. We dogs know that it's okay to be scared, especially about things like thunder, vacuum cleaners, and flashlights, but my dad didn't know this.

I taught him how to unearth his childlike self by projecting it onto me. He needed to be lovingly fooled into doing this for a few years before he could begin to realize that the love and affection he felt for me was really love and affection he had for the most sacred parts of himself. I helped him find what had been hopelessly lost and buried. It makes my tail wag when he sees less and less of the four-legged, brown, furry mirror that he's looking into and realizes more of his connection with who's looking into the mirror—his innocent inner child.

Tao of Vulnerability

When I was seven years old, I developed back problems. There were two reasons for this. First of all, I'm in a dachshund's body. It turns out that the talent Germans have for designing cars doesn't carry over into their engineering of the hybridized bodies of dogs. The main reason, though, was that I needed to develop a bad back *for my dad*. During these first seven years of my work with him, he made significant strides into his heart, emotions, innocence, and presence, but he was still only going paw-deep into it all. I knew he was finally ready to submerge to the depth of his heart; he needed to have the shell around his heart shattered with a lesson in vulnerability.

One Friday afternoon in the middle of the summer, I herniated a disk in my spine. It hurt way more than I thought it would! I was pacing around with my back arched trying to outrun the pain that I had initiated. It got Dad's attention. I could feel his heart fill with things he despised feeling: fear, sorrow, and helplessness. I could also see him trying to retreat into his head, thinking, "Maybe Zephyr just has an upset stomach, and this needs a little time to pass." It was no upset stomach! Those were always easy for my dad to recognize because I would surprise him with a puddle of vomit to step in. Oh! He would get so angry when my upset tummy taught him how mindful he wasn't being. But I digress . . .

After a half day of watching Dad fight the feelings in his heart by retreating into the rationalization-scape of his head, I decided enough was enough! I love him so much that I was willing to do whatever it took to help him crash deep into his heart, so I aggravated my herniated disk to the point my legs stopped working. It got the attention of the deepest of deep epicenters in his heart; he scooped me up immediately and took me on a middle-of-the-night ride to the emergency pet hospital. (Please note: although I don't ever recommend being vulnerable and driving, my dad got us there safely.) The shell broke open! Decades of emotional plaque liquefied, and my dad's heart came back to life. His tear ducts, which seemed cryogenically frozen for so long, were in full-fledged flow mode. While my body wasn't very happy and my legs weren't very hoppy, my spirit was hopping with happiness.

That weekend was filled with back surgery, morphine tripping (less vomiting than with ayahuasca, which is unfortunate), and the clinical smells of the pet hospital. While I hung out there for a few days, my dad spontaneously broke down crying at random times, becoming a puddle of pure, grade-A vulnerability. He was finally strong enough to feel weak and vulnerable. His obedience to his heart was improving. He was a good boy.

Tao of Neediness

When I got out of the hospital, I could barely stand, let alone walk. My dad had to do everything for me. I was needy because my dad needed me to be needy. He needed someone to model how to receive help because he didn't know how to accept it. He always denied his neediness so he could strategically stay disconnected from people, and he was goofy enough to call it "self-sufficiency." *Ha!* As a kid, he developed a bit of an allergy to his birthright to the kind of healthy need that facilitates human connection.

I was all too happy to let him carry me everywhere, do physical therapy on my legs and back, prepare special food, and cancel his appointments so he could be with me. I was showing him how okay I was with being needy. I've always been a glutton for attention, which made this an easy lesson for me to teach, but a hard one for my dad to learn.

It's been five years since my back surgery, and I've completely recovered. However, I'm no longer allowed to jump off the couch, in order to prevent further back issues. (I do have a little resentment about this. I always loved doing my Superman impression.) Despite this fact, every few months I do have a minor flare-up of pain. I teach from these episodes because Dad can still get a little too lost in living the unlived parts of his life, dancing with the devilish mistresses Shoulda, Woulda, and Coulda, who live in his head. These Minor Back Pain Teachings usually don't last longer than a few hours because my dad can now find his way back home to his heart through the scent trail of vulnerability pretty quickly these days.

Tao of Detachment

Even though my dad doesn't understand the sacred geometry of smells, he is smart enough to know that I won't be around forever. Based on his human arithmetic, he thinks I'm twelve years old, and he's coming to terms with how the infinite only chooses to inhabit a finite body for so long. He's seemingly grown wise enough to know that once he's learned all the lessons I came here to teach him, I too shall pass. I love Dad enough to be willing to leave him when he *needs* me to, not when he wants me to. If I stay longer than he needs me, then he'll forever continue to exclusively credit me for his gifts that I've taught him to discover, thinking that *I'm* the gift. If I'm always around when he feels his open, vulnerable heart, then it will be too easy for him to keep mistakenly thinking that *I'm* the gift. It's a bit of a Pavlov's Human Conditioning. I will leave when the time is right so he can fully own the gifts of himself that I've pointed him toward.

When the Student Is Ready

For now, I'll continue to carry my stuffed bunny into Dad's office when he's taking work, life, and himself too seriously. I'll squeak the hell out of it to remind him to be less attached and more playful, less certain and more curious, less rational and more feeling. I'll continue to lie on my back and rub his hand with my belly just to let him know that I care. I'll continue to take him on walks a couple times a day because he seems to love them so much. With each activity, his knowledge that every interaction is a fleeting blink of temporariness grows right along with his appreciation for our time together. When the student is ready, the master will disappear. When that time comes, I haven't decided yet if I'll take a one-way ride into the dream world at night or if I'll perhaps ask my dad for help taking my Earth leash off. If I do decide to ask, I know that he loves me enough to help.

Sniff on, my friends.

Zephyr

Zephyr's Advice for a Good Life

- If you love someone, show them your belly.

- Know that the world is overwhelmingly filled with love, except for vacuum cleaners—those are inherently evil.

- Now is always the right time for a treat.

- It's always Now.

- Two treats are better than one.

- Sleep on your back with all four paws in the air like you just don't care.

- Sniff everything and everyone; don't be afraid of intimacy.

- Don't not drool. It's bad manners.

- It's okay for humans to sit on the couch, too.

- Wake up to eat breakfast before taking your morning nap.

- Whenever vomiting, aim for the carpet.

- A toy without a squeaker is no toy at all.

- Help make the world a better place by chasing more tennis balls.

- A car ride with your head hanging out of the window can cure anything.

- People need a lot of guidance. Train them thoroughly. In fact, train them to think that they've trained you; it will help them be more obedient.

ABOVE Susan

LEFT Snoop Dogg at
wedding

Are You Willing
to Be a Fool for Love?

Susan Martin

Through play, spiritual energy can be sustained . . . Whether or not our rigid, mature minds reject play,
everything is still the display of the natural secret essence of the elements. . . .
If we have playmind, we can see through meditation that all phenomena are like magic.

Thinley Norbu Rinpoche, *Magic Dance*

What is a Happening? A game, an adventure, a number of activities
engaged in by participants for the sake of playing.

Alan Kaprow

On July 28, 2014, I married my dog. Surrounded by sixty friends and neighbors, I, Susan Martin, and Snoop Dogg Martin (no relation), tied the knot on the deck of our house overlooking the edge of a cliff at the end of a dirt road on a mesa in the middle of nowhere. Snoop and I had lived together for eight years and, more than just a companion, he quickly established himself as a focal point for lightness and humorous narratives. We composed songs together about current events. He has an email account: write him at snoopdoggmartin@gmail.com. He's on the mast-head of my website as part of the PR Team. His job description: *No matter the deadline or work-load, Snoop reminds staff and clients alike of Buddhism's Four Jewels: equanimity, lovingkindness, compassion, and joy!*

Are You Willing to Be a Fool for Love? was a Happening—a celebration of friendship, compan-ionship, and love. I had moved to the mesa in New Mexico years before from Los Angeles, and with friends on both coasts, Snoop and I noticed that most had never visited. In fact, it was out of frustra-tion that I declared to a friend in New York: "What do I have to do to get you to come? Get married?" The words were no sooner out of my mouth, when the lightbulb went on: *That's it. I'll marry Snoop Dogg!* The absurdity of the marriage metaphor struck our fancy as a way to entice friends who couldn't resist a destination wedding. "No one will be able to refuse a three-day Happening where guests become active participants in the foolishness," Snoop said.

The Save the Date read: "As in all great collaborations, Snoop and I need *you* to complete the picture. So, bring your sense of humor and play to the party." And they came: more than two dozen friends flew in from the far-flung corners of the world for the wedding.

Riffing on tradition, yet transgressive and unconventional, the wedding was a chance for us to express our creativity and tribal connection. Snoop's favorite expression, "Wow! Bow-wow!" became our clarion call. Snoop and I discovered there is no place on Earth where it is *legal* to marry a dog (or any animal for that matter). However, we did uncover a handful of people who, like us, have defied reason and convention: A woman fell in love with a snake and was married to it at a traditional Hindu wedding celebrated by two thousand guests; a Sudanese man was caught having sex with a neighbor's goat (nicknamed "Rose") and was ordered by the council of elders to pay a dowry and marry the animal; and the Cheyenne myth, "The Girl Who Married a Dog," tells how a group of seven stars known as the Pleiades originated from seven puppies that a Cheyenne chief's daughter gave birth to after mysteriously being visited by a dog in human form to whom she vowed, "Wherever you go, I go."

It took us six months to prepare for the big event. Each guest was greeted with a necklace of dog tags: a red hydrant was engraved with "Love," a gold heart with "Friends," and a bone with our names and the date of the ceremony. For sixty goody bags of local favors, I gathered "lady sage" from along the Chama River to make into sacred bundles and rocks from the dazzling array in the arroyo. There were door prizes including a portable dog sculpture; special performances by the Rough Rubies, who sang lonesome cowboy songs by a faux campfire; Hattie Hathaway's electrifying performance of "State of Independence;" and a soundtrack of more than a hundred songs featuring dogs. Everyone who came had their choice of every species of squeaky toy imaginable—from hedgehogs and pigs to bunnies and skunks (more on that later).

We hosted a rehearsal dinner for out-of-towners in a miniscule restaurant in the tiny village of El Rito, complete with speeches by Snoop's best man and by my maid of honor, Danielle, who was with me the day Snoop and I met. The mother of the groom, Jane Friedman—a proud, straight-as-an-arrow New York Jewish woman—gave the marriage her blessing: "Years ago Susan and I established criteria for what we wanted in a partner, including, as I remember: someone in the next room who'd be a soul mate, someone to take a walk with in the night air and through the winter snow, someone to play with, and someone to love. So it is without reservation that I welcome her into my Snoop's life."

Love lasts forever.

(If you're wondering, Snoop's father was a hound/heeler mix who shall remain nameless. Jane does not kiss and tell.)

Late Saturday afternoon, surrounded by friends, Snoop and I stood under the "hoopla" adorned with tulle and ribbons and bows and local critters culled from the party store (snakes, tarantulas, birds, and worms). As "Walkin' the Dog" by Rufus Thomas played, we were married by Marquita and blessed by Dexter, the ceremonial leader of the village of Abiquiu.

My vows were easy to write: "Over the last nine years you have given me joy and lovingkindness every single day. You are not a person, but you are a friend. You set an example by your presence and your equanimity. Your pace becomes my pace, and our rambles are the occasion for my most creative flights of fancy. Thank you, Snoop, for coming to me and thank you for bringing together all these wonderful people in celebration of friendship and love." Snoop's vows, which he texted to his best man to read, began, "First thing: get down on all fours." And I did. Rather than a ring, in keeping with his namesake, Snoop Doggy Dogg, we exchanged bling. With the ceremony complete, each guest was asked to feel the love by squeezing their squeaky toys in a cacophony of sound that caused the groom to go slightly crazy.

Our marriage has been a happy one. Snoop's sensitivity and calm abiding spirit continue to nurture me and give me joy. And did I mention his eyes? Deep, soulful, almost human.

Now, in four short years, he's gone from built-like-a-brick-house protector dog to frail, old being. An animal once so independent and strong, with a life of his own as well as with me, is now blind and deaf and completely dependent. I'm feeling deeply the cruel genetic truth, the cosmic joke, the inevitable: that in spite of our deep and abiding love for our beloved dogs, they are going to die. Love and Mortality inextricably bound together. Yet as human beings—in spite of this knowing, the grief, the loneliness, the longing—we choose again and again to go to that well of love.

A little while ago, Snoop got really sick. It was touch and go. All I could do was give back to him what he had so unfailingly given to me. Together we composed a song that I sang over and over to him in the silence of our home until he recovered. It goes like this:

> Snoop Dogg, Susie
> We'll be together
> Snoop Dogg, good dog
> Love lasts forever.
> (Repeat.)

ABOVE Gita

LEFT Lola and Mirabai

Dog Angels

Mirabai Starr

My daughter Jenny sent a team of dog angels to my rescue after she was gone. They did not always act angelically. Hobbes died. Ziggy bit people, and then died. Isaiah shot like a nova across the horizon of our hearts for five years, and then he disappeared. Dying angels are not exactly my prescription for healing, but they each seemed to fulfill their appointed task—prior to and because of their untimely deaths.

When I first got together with Jeff, he made it clear that he was not interested in adding a dog to the family, and the subject did not arise again. But after Jenny died, I did not know what to do with all the nurturing energy I had been accustomed to pouring onto my child. My heart was a teacup, and my love was hot tea filling up and spilling over, scorching my hand and soaking my clothes. Drenched and burning, I turned my thoughts to a puppy.

Jeff agreed to a scouting trip to the animal shelter, and we came home with a four-month-old German/Australian shepherd mix whom we named Hobbes, in honor of Jenny's favorite philosopher—not Thomas Hobbes, the stuffy British social theorist, but Calvin's imaginary sidekick of cartoon fame. Hobbes punctuated my bouts of leaden despair with moments of unalloyed joy. He was devoted from the beginning and seemed to know exactly how to tend my heart. The one and only day he found his way off our property, he was hit by a car a few yards away from our house and bled to death beneath a statue of Saint Francis that Father Bill had placed in his front yard next door. I concluded that Saint Francis had sent Hobbes to get me through the most arduous leg of my grief journey, and that when his work was done he had moved on to minister to some other broken-hearted mother. But I wouldn't survive another loss. No more dogs.

A few months later, however, I found myself driving to the animal shelter in a trance and returning with the most ridiculous-looking little creature I had ever seen—a mix of about a dozen radically different breeds, but predominantly blue heeler and Chihuahua. He had black-and-white speckles, a pink belly, and an exaggerated underbite. We named him Ziggy. Our newest family member alternated between dissolving into blissful sleep in our arms and periodically snapping at our faces with no provocation. Ziggy, too, managed to slip out of the yard and collide with a car driving far too fast on our rural road. We buried him next to Hobbes.

My yearning for another dog was proportionate to my missing Jenny. I sat with that. I let it burn. And then one day the phone rang.

"Hi, honey, it's your friend Elaine," said my friend Elaine. "What are you doing?"

"Reading," I lied. I was sleeping. A bereaved father named Alan told me that when his son was killed in a car accident his boss had asked him if he was having trouble sleeping, and Alan had answered that no, it was being awake he was having trouble with. Me, too.

"Can you meet me at Cid's?" Cid's was our local natural foods store, a place I had been avoiding because I knew at least 50 percent of the people who shopped there, and everybody seemed to have a different story they told themselves about my loss. "There is an adorable basket of puppies in the parking lot. The guy says he's going to drown whichever ones are left at the end of the day."

"That is so not fair, Elaine. How can I possibly say no?"

"You can't. Look, I'll get one and you get one. That way, when you travel I can take care of your puppy, and when I go away you can take mine. Our dogs will be sisters!" That was a good idea, actually. "There's this tiny one with pale-green eyes and freckles. She looks like you."

"Oh, great."

"How soon can you be here? I'll wait."

Never, I should have said. *I can't love another being. I have nothing left.* Besides, I'd promised Jeff. Our dog days were over.

"Twenty minutes."

"Great, I'll be the lady with a puppy in each arm."

And so it was that Gita came into my life. Gita, my special-needs dog, who had one thing and another wrong with her from the moment she crept in the door and rushed to hide under the bed: a broken tail, inexplicable fevers, skin irritations. She was afraid of everything, and I developed a palette of behaviors to accommodate her anxieties. Yet once I had earned Gita's trust, she venerated me with singular devotion, and she read my thoughts so effortlessly that any training was redundant. Elaine's dog, Ramona, succumbed to one of the same mysterious illnesses that struck Gita, but Gita lived on.

After Ramona's death, Gita was depressed. Her coat grew dull, and she was no longer interested in taking walks.

"She needs a companion," I said.

"Oy vey," said Jeff, but it was difficult to disagree.

It was embarrassing to go to the shelter for the third time, with two dead dogs on our record. But this time we had a foolproof containment system. We installed an expensive "invisible fence" with shock collars. Our new puppy, whom we named Isaiah after the prophet of peace, had the system beat within a week. But he lasted five years. Isaiah was by far the most beautiful of all my dog angels. He had long, golden-red fur and eyes like chocolate stars. He was enthusiastic, tender, and hopelessly untrainable. Isaiah adored Gita, and she made a show of putting up with his affections. But after Isaiah disappeared one cold December night while Jeff and I were out to dinner, Gita mourned him as fiercely as I did.

It took us a year to say yes to *another* dog. On the day that Jenny would have turned twenty-five, we adopted Lola, an accidental mix of two show dogs: a keeshond and a German pinscher. Lola bounded into the house, plopped down on Jeff's feet, and gazed up into his face. Then, as if shot out of a cannon, she bounced from one corner of the house to another before collapsing on the floor and falling asleep. Terrified, smitten, we welcomed Lola into the family, where she began entertaining us with her cleverness, driving us crazy with her hyperactivity, and melting our hearts with her kindness.

Gita grew old, little by little letting go of this life, and sank into a slow pool of quietude. For her final year she abided in a liminal space, bedraggled and addled, incontinent and even more withdrawn than usual. Yet she seemed to be incapable of relinquishing the loving care we lavished on her and slipping into death of her own accord. Life in a body was no fun, but it wasn't all bad either. It involved canned lamb, a soft bed, and a steady flow of adoration delicately dispensed.

Toward the end I took to kneeling beside Gita and whispering in her ear as if I had a secret for her alone to ponder: "Whenever you're ready, my love, you can go. I'm alright now." And I was. But Gita kept on living, even as her skin became a battleground of abscesses and her internal organs revolted.

Jeff and I agreed that the most loving thing we could do was to have Gita put to sleep. As it turned out, our vet, Trisha, had been waiting a long time for us to reach this conclusion. She showed up at our house on a sweet summer morning with two syringes: one to calm Gita and the other to stop her heart.

We had prepared for a gentle, sacred passing. I made a playlist of the music I wanted to accompany my eccentric soulmate across the threshold of this life: "Calling All Angels" by Jane Siberry with k.d. lang; "Baba Hanuman" by Krishna Das; "Song of Keening" sung by Áine Minogue. We bought a soft, purple blanket in which to wrap her body. The house was tidy, a candle burned in a tall blue glass, and jasmine incense smoke curled into the air. Jeff and our nephew Nick had dug a grave the day before, and we promised our family we'd call them once Gita had died so they could join us for her burial.

When Trisha walked in, Gita hobbled away from her and wedged herself between the couch and the coffee table. She looked up at the vet, then glanced at me, then turned her gaze to Jeff. "You're okay, Gita," he said, and she noticeably relaxed. Trisha knelt and administered the first shot into Gita's hip. Within a minute her eyes began to drift closed.

"Wait!" I said, as if it were possible to reverse the course we had set. "I want her to die in her own bed." Jeff and Trisha lifted Gita and carried her the few feet to her sheepskin, on which we had laid out the purple blanket so that we could easily swaddle her body when it was over. I sat beside her and wrapped my arms around her. I pressed my face against her face and murmured, "I love you, my sweet Gita."

The voices of Siberry and lang soared: "Calling all angels, calling all angels / Walk me through this one, don't leave me alone."

Trisha bent down and injected Gita with the second dose. I began to cry. She placed her stethoscope on Gita's side and closed her eyes. She nodded. It was done. The whole procedure lasted less than five minutes.

"I've never seen a dog so ready to go," Trisha said. She stood up and smiled. "And I've never been part of such a beautiful death. Thank you." She hugged me. "Thank you." She hugged Jeff.

> The presence of my dog gave me just enough courage to stay present in the fire of my grief.

I didn't have a chance to say goodbye to my daughter. I didn't get to accompany her to the Other World on the wings of Kirtan and Celtic lamentations. I wasn't given the opportunity to tell her I loved her one last time. Jenny's death shattered every bone in my soul, and Gita's death helped mend me a little.

Lola mourned Gita for weeks. Our generally bouncy little dog curled up on my office rug and stayed there. Every few minutes she would lift her eyebrows and let out a heart-wrenching sigh. It was as if missing Gita were a physical torment for Lola. We showered her with tenderness, and little by little she rejoined the stream of life, but Lola had been changed by Gita's death. Her goofy clamor gave way to a more gracious stillness. She seemed to absorb some of Gita's preternatural ability to see into my soul. Eventually Lola settled into her status as Only Dog with good-natured resignation, and now I believe she relishes it.

Sometimes when Jeff and Lola and I are hiking up the ridge behind our house in the Sangre de Cristo foothills, I miss Gita. I yearn for her the way a grown woman might wish she could still curl up in bed with her wise grandmother, gone a dozen years now, and confide the confusions of her romantic escapades or get some advice about a career change. Gita's was a long life, filled with adventures in the wilderness and a cozy home. The presence of my dog gave me just enough courage to stay present in the fire of my grief for my child, a fire that continues to transfigure the landscape of my soul. Only now I can breathe again, and the air is filled with light.

ABOVE Lady and Myotai Sensei

Here for You

Bonnie Myotai Treace Sensei

'd spent a week writing in the high woods. A friend of a friend's North Carolina cabin came complete with "loaner" dog, complete with, shall we say, a "plenitude" of rooster, chicken, and bear decorations and enough personal items in every otherwise-immaculate room that the creepy feeling of having borrowed someone's shoes was constant. Even the poor dog struck me as one of those too-long-in-boarding vacant souls: anyone will do, throw my ball, food please. I had the mild headache I'd had for six months, and it was time to drive on toward Asheville.

Something I later learned: the road from where I was to where I was headed is known as The Black Mountain Rag, named for an old fiddle tune about the dark-green Lauada firs that give the Black Mountains their name. In musical terms, a "rag" is a tune with multiple twists and curves up and down the scales. Those who do not have a headache of mysterious origin that makes them seasick describe the road this way: "a scenic route that twists and turns through the mountains like the music itself." Crawling out of the rental car at the first place I saw, I checked into a small hotel and put my head under the cool, dark cave of a pillow to stop the spinning. It would be a while until I connected with the music of the mountain roads.

I called my relatives and assured them I needed another day or so "to write" and not to worry, because the headache thing was already a concern to the family circle. Did they believe I was that taken with the little town I'd pulled into? Or could they more rightly sense I just physically could not drive the fifteen miles farther and then have conversations, or be in rooms where lights were on and where there might be a shriek of happiness from a grandchild who would—I don't know—cause my head to explode?

Something had to happen, I knew that. After my second bout with Lyme disease and my supposed recovery the year prior, I'd been a different sort of person. I knew that it was even odd that I thought the lack of connection with the "loaner" dog was an issue with the dog: never in my life had I been unable to sense the heart of an animal. That my impulse was not to take responsibility—to examine what was going on with me and what was possible—was very out of character and had begun with this headache, then continued evolving. I knew the mystery of what was "out of order" physically had to get a better quality of intelligent attention medically, but along the way I had to find the way to re-energize my spiritual life. This was the challenge I gave myself each day and was what I was walking with the next morning in Black Mountain. It was on that walk that I saw the sign "English Springers Here for You."

A woman named Heather had set up in someone's front yard on Cherry Street with eight puppies and several older dogs. I went into the tea shop next door and bought a bag of cookies. "May I lie on the ground and let your puppies jump on me?" I asked. "I can't buy a dog, but I did bring irresistible cookies." She laughed, and after a few minutes of heavenly rolling about with the brood, I sat with Heather on the steps drinking glasses of iced tea. As what turned out to be a couple hours of conversation continued, one of her "mother dogs" took up residence by my side, eventually going to sleep on my feet.

I told Heather that ever since working as Zen clergy with the Red Cross at the Family Assistance Center after 9/11, I'd had a dream of someday having a dog to work with. I'd been involved with debriefing clergy at the end of very difficult days, and I would sometimes point to all we could learn from the therapy dogs. They would position themselves near someone in tremendous pain, with no illusion that they had some wise-enough word to say, and often I'd see a moment when the barrier would fall. A hand would reach out; comfort would be given and received. No barrier, no anxiety about sufficiency. Just love.

Heather said, "I've never seen her like this." The mother dog was looking up at me. I looked back into her eyes. I had a fleeting, disorienting glimmer of feeling like my old, pre-headache self, which made me both want to steal the dog and run for my life. Too strange. Long story short: of course the girl gets the dog. I did explain that I could not possibly take one of the breeding dogs. Heather, it turns out, a good Southern lady, believed the Lord had a plan and this dog and I were part of it. I explained that I genuinely had no money for a dog. But then the friend who had arranged the cabin loan called to check on me, heard the story, loved it, and immediately wired the funds to buy said dog, with vet care for a year. By the end of the day, it was somehow natural as air to continue the drive toward my visit in Asheville—Lady and I sharing a chicken sandwich in the car.

> Dog eyes, enlightened eyes: what happens when we stop dividing things, ourselves— enough and not enough, life and death?

Over the next several years, I would travel to the Mayo Clinic, have surgery to remove a tumor, get a chance to reshape my work, and go on many, many walks with the "English Springer Who is Here for Me." In the beginning, because I was spending a good deal of time with bags of frozen peas on my quite sore head and trying to keep my nonprofit afloat while sometimes only managing to leave the bed for a few hours a day, Lady was my attendant of sorts. I noticed she had an uncommon sense of humor for a dog, which came in handy on days when drama and darkness knocked at the door. Suddenly there she'd be at the top of the staircase I had no interest in climbing, insisting with a woof that I play "Are You the Dog That Gives Me Pause?" At which point she would thrust her paws over the top stair and howl. Okay. I will cheer up. Okay.

As I got to feeling stronger, Lady indeed got certified as a therapy dog and has had a big life, sleeping on many people's feet along the way, offering her belly for rubs, and being a gentle and generous friend to hundreds of kids, seniors, folks in hospitals, and every other person walking down the street.

Lady never fails, though, to let me know I'm her One. If I get up in the morning and start the business of the day without first attending to a real "Hello, glad we're together! Isn't it grand?" she reminds me. The wider question stands: how to carry that into all relations, even the ones not as rewarding or softly furred. If she's been with many people for several hours, I'll get the look that says, "Let's head home; I'm not a retriever, after all." This is our private joke. When she got her therapy-dog certification, the official said to keep an eye out for when she tires of working; she is, after all, "not a retriever." It is also my shorthand for acknowledging that with the pain pattern I still deal with, I'm not so much a retriever anymore either. (Is anyone?) Meeting that with dog eyes—no barrier, no anxiety about sufficiency, just love—might change everything.

Lady has been on what they call "the last stretch of trail" for a while: nasal cancer. The vets say she won't see next year. Motto of the house these days is "Every day is a good day," in the same spirit of teaching as Zen Master Yunmen's of long ago. Dog eyes, enlightened eyes: what happens when we stop dividing things, ourselves—enough and not enough, life and death?

ABOVE   Abby

TOP RIGHT   Bentley

MIDDLE RIGHT   Chris

BOTTOM RIGHT   Onyx

Unconditional Loving-Acceptance (Even on Our Worst Days)

Chris Grosso

D runk, I fell down onto the kitchen floor, mad at myself, mad at my life, and sick of what I believed to be a completely stupid fucking world. My feelings of anger, despair, and broken-ness shattered when they were met by the unconditional loving-acceptance of my three dogs. Sitting on that wooden floor, not quite blackout drunk but well on my way, I looked into the eyes of Abby (a brown and white bassett hound), Onyx (a black bloodhound/Labrador mix), and Bentley (a black and gray mini-dachshund). As I did, I realized that I wasn't experiencing the judgment or disappointment that I was used to from people—myself included—after relapsing with drugs and alcohol. Instead, what I saw in my three dogs was joy: boundless, free, spirited joy. Not only did I *see* their joy, more importantly, I *felt* their unconditional, perfect, loving-acceptance. In that drunken, broken, and self-deprecatory moment, it was almost too much to bear.

I wish I could say that experience of unconditional canine loving-acceptance resulted in an incredible awakening for me—one in which I was inspired to put down the drugs and booze once and for all. I wish I could say that I didn't continue to drink myself into a blackout state that night and wake up the next morning feeling horribly sick and anxious while staring at an empty bottle of vodka on top of my copy of Chuck Klosterman's *Sex, Drugs, and Cocoa Puffs* as the withdrawals began to set in. I wish I could say that, but I can't.

What I can say is that, thanks to my connection to Abby, Onyx, and Bentley, as well as the relationships I'd had with the other dogs up to that point in my life (Bowser, Mocha, and Sam), no matter how broken I felt or how terribly tragic life seemed, I knew as a direct result of my connection with them that there was in fact such a thing as unconditional love. It was the kind of love I'd later read about in books by some of the great wisdom teachers like Jesus, Thich Nhat Hanh, Rumi, or hell, even author Charles Bukowski in his gentler moments.

It is in this undeniable knowing that I've often found the strength to pick myself back up after the numerous rock bottoms I've hit—the times when my experience of the world seemed particularly jarring, distant, and chaotic. Because no matter how strange or difficult things became, my dogs had shown me that there was such a thing as *real, authentic* love. Of course, our family and friends can show us a very deep, authentic love, one that is borderline unconditional. But in human relationships, there are always going to be disappointments, anger, frustration, opinions, and judgments. It's not that these things are necessarily bad, but they do place certain conditions on our human relationships, regardless of how much we'd like to think we can love unconditionally. So to say human love is just as unconditional as a dog's—no matter how very close it may be, which in my own case has been as close as it can possibly get with my family's love and support—isn't entirely accurate.

Dogs love for love's sake and nothing else—no strings attached. It's the kind of love that doesn't depend on a single thing, the kind of love that accepts us as the flawed and fucked-up humans that we are. And it's the kind of unconditional loving-acceptance that will always be there eagerly awaiting us when we return home.

That is, of course, until it's not.

Every loss of a dog I've lived through has been incredibly difficult, as I'm sure it has been for anyone reading this book. Yet (and at the risk of sounding clichéd), during those heartbreakingly crushing times I've found that there's also the potential for very real insight, gratitude, and compassion.

In 2014, Abby died. Six months before her passing, I had an experience that made the aforementioned insight, gratitude, and compassion manifest. Abby had been sick with various stomach issues, but on this particular morning, she was sicker than I'd ever seen her. She was sprawled on the kitchen floor in virtually the same exact place—and eerily in the same exact position—where just two years earlier Onyx had passed away.

Abby's breathing was labored, and she could barely open her eyes. As I sat down with her, she tried to get up, only to fall, after which she gave up and went back to her shallow breathing. Sitting there alone with Abby that morning, I cried the hardest I'd cried since Onyx died. With my heart breaking into a million pieces, I began to thank Abby for being such an amazing dog, for all the wonderful memories she'd given me, and for the unconditional loving-acceptance she'd shown me no matter how out-of-control my life had become. As I continued mustering words to express how much she meant to me, I gradually became aware that even though a storm of emotions thrashed within me, I was still present in the moment—present with the heartbreak, present with the tears, present with the feelings of complete hollowness. I realized that my heart, while hurting terribly, was open to the entire experience, and my mind filled with an equanimity that I could only credit to years of meditation practice and learning to compassionately lean into the pain rather than run away from it.

> Unconditional love *is* real, and we're *all* deserving of it.

As tears streamed down my face, a memory came to mind from when I'd attended a Medicine Buddha ceremony performed by the Venerable Khensur Rinpoche Lobsang Tenzin at Chenrezig Tibetan Buddhist Center in Middletown, Connecticut. Within the Mahayana Buddhist tradition there are numerous Buddhas that represent different aspects of Buddha-nature—compassion, emptiness, and wisdom. The Medicine Buddha represents healing. It's believed that by invoking the Medicine Buddha's name or reciting the Medicine Buddha's mantra, we receive spiritual, psychological, and physical healing.

Some say that even *hearing* the mantra recited just once can provide someone with a good rebirth or reincarnation. During the ceremony I attended, Rinpoche, who is from Tibet and received the

Medicine Buddha transmission directly from His Holiness the Fourteenth Dalai Lama, taught us the mantra: *Tayata Om Bhekandze Bhekandze Maha Bhekanzde Randza Samungate Soha.*

It was in hope of a good rebirth that I began reciting the words aloud for Abby:

Tayata Om Bhekandze Bhekandze Maha Bhekanzde
Randza Samungate Soha. Tayata Om Bhekandze
Bhekandze Maha Bhekanzde Randza Samungate Soha.
Tayata Om Bhekandze Bhekandze Maha Bhekanzde
Randza Samungate Soha. Tayata Om Bhekandze
Bhekandze Maha Bhekanzde Randza Samungate Soha.

The mantra breaks down as: *Tayata,* which means "gone beyond" (beyond Samsara and Nirvana). *Om* represents the jewel holder, the wish-fulfilling and auspicious one. When we say *Bhekandze Bhekandze* we're calling the Medicine Buddha twice. *Maha Bhekandze* represents the greatness of the Medicine Buddha. *Randza Samungate* translates to "perfectly liberated or awakened." And *Soha* means "dissolve in me."

As I repeated these words, tears still falling down my cheeks, I became aware of increasing peace and acceptance arising around the situation. With my mother's help, I wrapped Abby in a blanket and took her to the vet's office. When we arrived, I believed these would be my final moments with Abby. A technician brought us into a room, and I set our dog on the floor while we waited for the vet. After about five minutes, for no apparent reason, Abby stood up! She began to walk around and even wagged her tail.

She was still weak in her back legs and hobbled a bit, but she was up and moving. As completely overjoyed as I was, I still found what was happening to be extremely weird, like David Lynch's *Blue Velvet* weird. My mother and I looked at one another and didn't know what to make of it. I was scared to get my hopes up because none of this made any sense. The vet came in a few minutes later, and she didn't know what to make of it either. She took Abby to get X-rays, which showed that everything was fine with her insides. The vet drew blood to have it tested, and the results came back clear.

For the following six months, Abby was back to as normal as a twelve-year-old dog could be.

I don't want anyone to get the wrong idea here and think that I attribute her miraculous recovery to my reciting the Medicine Buddha mantra (although, *hey*—you never know). The point is that through the recitation of the Medicine Buddha mantra while faced with what seemed like dire circumstances with Abby, a sense of peace, calm, and spacious acceptance arose around the heartbreak I was experiencing. In retrospect, I know it wasn't a coincidence that the Medicine Buddha mantra popped into my head in that moment, and since then it's one that I've brought back into a more regular rotation in my practice: for myself, for Abby, Onyx, Bentley, Mocha, Sam, Bowser, and for all beings everywhere.

It is my sincerest wish that, even during our worst days, we *all* come to see ourselves in the same unconditional loving light that our beautiful tail-wagging friends see us. Unconditional love *is* real, and we're *all* deserving of it. All of us—and that includes you, too!

ABOVE Maya and Eckhart

Light through Tapestry

Eckhart Tolle

*E*ckhart Tolle often speaks of his love and appreciation for dogs—or as he calls them, "the guardians of Being"—illuminating the reciprocal nature of the human-canine relationship. By living with humans, he explains, dogs grow in consciousness; for us, dogs offer the opportunity to relate to another being with an open heart and without judgment.

For ten years Eckhart enjoyed the companionship of Maya, a Cavalier King Charles spaniel, who was an instant friend to virtually everyone she met. The following contribution is drawn from an exchange between Eckhart and a retreat participant struggling with the recent death of her dog.

What is the source of the love we feel for our dogs? Of course we love to touch our dogs, to hold them, to feel the dog's aliveness. But what we really love in the dog we can't see. Ultimately, what we love in the dog is not the external form; we love in the dog that which has *no form*—the underlying consciousness that is the indestructible essence of all life. To realize shared consciousness is love in the true sense.

To simply watch a dog without any kind of mental commentary—to just tune in—provides a link to the present moment, because the dog keeps you in touch with the innermost core of Being that is beyond the mind. You can look into the eyes of a dog and see that innermost core. There are teachings that say every being is a spark of the divine, of God. You can often see that spark more clearly in dogs than in a human being because the human has the veil of mind, negative emotions, and ego that gets in the way.

When we experience the death of a dog, it is painful; there may be tears and sadness as you witness the dissolution of a cherished life form. Yet in the moment of death and perhaps for a little bit after, this dissolution leaves behind an open space in you—the space of what I call the *formless*.

Imagine your life as a tapestry, and one aspect of the tapestry is the dog. The tapestry shows you petting the dog and feeling love for the dog. Suddenly you're looking at this tapestry and the dog begins to dissolve. What's happening to the dog? You were just there petting the dog, and suddenly there's an empty space in that tapestry. That's very painful. The form has dissolved.

But what is it that gives life to this whole tapestry? It is the light of the formless that shines through all forms—a light that becomes obstructed by the forms but can still shine through somehow. So when a form has dissolved, if you concentrate on the lack of what was there that was so lovely, you get stuck on that level. But if you look more deeply, then you see that where that form was there's actually more light shining through now. That happens when you completely surrender to the fact of death, whether the death of a human being or a dog or any form of life.

When you completely surrender to the fact of death, you experience more than just the sadness over the dissolution of the form; you also sense a deepening in yourself because you sense that where the form was, the light now shines through more fully. This is why death is ultimately always sacred. Why? Because when the form dissolves, the formless can shine through more strongly. That can be transformative in you, but it requires surrender to the fact of death.

For the animal, death is easier. The animal can surrender into it, although, yes, there is a will to live. But the animal can surrender; surrender is the key.

Ultimately, we're talking about the realization of something in you that's beyond death, and that is what you loved in the dog—what you still love. And that cannot go away.

When we must say goodbye to a dog, we can let it become a transformative experience and, yes, let the tears still flow if they flow; there's nothing wrong with that. But surrender to the fact of death and realize that only the form dies. That which gives life to the form is not subject to decay or death; you can sense that in yourself. And then you can sense it in the dog. And then the death of the dog is not as heavy as it would be if you equated the essence of the dog with the form of the dog.

> When the form dissolves, the formless can shine through more strongly.

So what you love in the dog is the dog's consciousness, which ultimately is one with your consciousness. It is life itself: a beautiful expression—temporary, of course—of the One life. And we can honor that and be grateful for that.

ABOVE   Lala (front), Hermes, and Sera

My Furry Soulbody

Sera Beak

I t was Lala's soul that drew me to her before her body.

I wanted to adopt a large dog, but when I walked into San Francisco's Animal Care and Control, Lala's part-Chihuahua, part-who-knows-what dark eyes were the first ones to meet mine. Unlike most of the shelter dogs I saw that day, Lala wouldn't look away. She looked and looked *and looked* into me until my big-dog dreams dissolved. If the eyes are the window to the soul, then Lala gave me an unfiltered view into hers.

"Shit," I gently muttered in defeat. "I guess you're mine."

Lala refused to be treated like a small dog. She jumped out of any bag I tried to carry her in and ripped through *two* "indestructible" pet carriers midflight. (She's currently on a major airline's "no fly" list.) She dominated every park we visited. People watched with astonishment as Lala faced off with rottweilers and left greyhounds in the dust. She even managed to uproot the oldest, laziest, and fattest dogs who chased her with floppy glee.

Back then, Lala was awesomely agile and ridiculously brave, and she demonstrated moves that would put a martial artist to shame. She raced up cliffs, leapt over boulders, climbed trees (I kid you not), spun through the air, and could snatch a piece of fried chicken off a stranger's picnic blanket before you could blink.

She was so *very* alive.

* * *

The dharma between Lala and me blossomed after I met Marion Woodman, a Jungian psychoanalyst whose work centers on the embodiment of the soul.

I had the honor of interviewing Marion for a documentary about the Divine Feminine, and it was during this interview that I realized that I was completely *disembodied*.

Years of spiritual study and transcendent practice, a chronic case of psychological avoidance, and a history of soul trauma resulted in me not fully inhabiting my body. I was detached from my physical form and feelings, disconnected from my somatic awareness, primal instincts, and honest human needs. My attention was up and out, not down and in. I floated above this planet instead of sinking my heels into the ground.

In other words, I was *not* so very alive.

This painful recognition shook me to the core, and my life fell to pieces as a result. I lost my intimate relationship, my career, many close friends, my spiritual beliefs, and a sense of meaning and purpose.

It was soon after this cataclysmic interview that Lala started to sleep in my bed. One emotional night after I turned off the light, I felt a soft weight land on the mattress and pad toward me. Then, with impressive determination, Lala used her entire head to forcefully lift my heavy blanket so she could scoot her petite body underneath it.

Lift, scoot, lift, scoot, lift, scoot.

When Lala reached the bottom of the bed, she collapsed in a heap on top of my feet. It was oddly comforting to have a nine-pound sack of warm fur weighing me down. I stopped crying and started breathing deeper.

Throughout the night, Lala moved her animal body up the entire length of my human body: my calves, my thighs, my hips, my belly, my chest. When I awoke the next morning, her head was resting on my pillow, her body tucked under the covers, and she stared deep into my eyes, as if communicating:

This is your body.
Be in it.
You are part animal,
like me.

No matter how painful things became during this dark time in my life, no matter how lost and confused I felt, I knew that every night I would receive a reminder to be in my body, a healing for my soul, and a *transmission of Life* from this rough-and-tough little mutt who, I swear, knew exactly what she was doing.

I started paying closer attention to Lala during the day. I noticed how unselfconscious she was—steeped in the present moment, attentive to her surroundings and needs—and, of course, how she acted instinctually. If she wanted something, she went for it. If she didn't like the vibe, she walked away. If something startled her, she shook it off. If someone approached too fast or broke her (or my) boundaries, she growled at them and guarded me. She didn't second-guess herself. She didn't temper her natural responses or worry what others might think. She did what she did. She was what she was. And if other people or dogs didn't like it, so be it.

These were *vital* teachings for me, not only because I was a disembodied, spiritual bypasser—someone who uses spirituality to escape the human experience—but also because I was a good girl, ultra-polite, a people pleaser.

One time, Lala refused to let a man I was dating enter our apartment. She barked, growled, and even charged at him. I was mortified and apologetic. I scolded Lala and shoved her into the bedroom where she proceeded to howl and slam her little body into the door until the guy grew so uneasy he decided to leave. I didn't blame him, but I did blame Lala. A few weeks later, I learned that this person had a history of mistreating the women he dated. I was shocked and then ashamed. I imme-diately broke things off with him, apologized to Lala, and gave her an extra-long belly rub and chewy treat for acting like the fiercely protective animal she was . . . and that I needed to become.

After this event, I started to imitate Lala. Instead of just tossing her a ball or giving her a squeaky toy, I started to crawl around on the ground with her. When we played tug-of-war with a rope, we *both* growled ferociously and flexed our muscles. When I was scared or stressed, I shook my body to release the excess energy. When I was in social situations, I noticed and practiced meeting my own needs instead of getting overrun by the needs of others. When I walked through the city alone, I paid closer attention to my surroundings and took extra precautions to keep myself safe. And, I became *much* more discerning of the people I invited into my home and into my life.

On our daily outings to Buena Vista Park, I inhaled the multitude of rich scents and eagerly explored the stunning topography with Lala. I scrambled over tree trunks, huffed and puffed up hills, cut new trails, and flopped down on the grass in order to soak up the sun. I would lie there on the earth—my body humming and my senses buzzing—gratefully absorbing Life. Lala loved it when I played with her like this and did her absolute best to encourage it. If I got buried in work or didn't feel like going out, she would bark until I grabbed her leash. If I lagged behind in the park or at the beach, she circled back and rounded me up. If I was disconnected or lost in my thoughts, she jumped up and bounced off my body with her paws.

Be here with me. Be wild with me. Be alive with me.

Lala began showing up in my dreams as a symbol of my soulbody. If she was happy and playful and had a thick coat of shiny fur, I knew I was doing well. If she was lost or starving, mangy or hurt, I knew I had some serious work to do in the morning.

About three years after adopting Lala, I attended a weekend spiritual workshop offered by a teacher I had regularly studied with before my interview with Marion Woodman. However, on the first day of the retreat, I began to feel oppressed and caged—like I wanted to get the hell out of there. I brushed these negative feelings aside, viewing them as typical inner blocks to my spiritual development.

Later that night, I dreamt that Lala was being sodomized by the spiritual teacher leading the retreat! In the dream, I didn't pause. I forcefully broke down a door, threw the teacher to the ground, and rescued my poor dog.

I'd like to say that I left the retreat the next day, but I can't because I didn't. Shedding domestication and growing thick soulskin takes time. However, I did get the memo, for I have used the potent lesson of that dream to gauge every spiritual event I have attended or held since. Now, I regularly walk away from people or environments that do not respect or make allowances for my soulbody. I often ask myself, "What would Lala do?" And, more recently, "What would Hermes do?"

I adopted Hermes, my other magnificent and mysterious Chihuahua concoction, six years after Lala. She lets him know every single day that she was mine first. Hermes is just fine with Lala's dominance as long as he can snuggle and snort with me every chance he can get. Lala is serious, and Hermes is carefree. Lala obeys, and Hermes is mischievous. Lala is my dharma protector, and Hermes is my dharma goofball—he keeps me laughing and from taking this whole embodiment gig too seriously. These two sandwich my body every night. The feminine Lala is a sleek seal that softly glides against my skin, whereas the masculine Hermes is a beefy linebacker who crashes into me at every possible angle—a linebacker who snores, farts, and sleeps with his tongue sticking out. I feel balanced and blessed between them both.

Remember, you are not so different from us.

Perhaps the greatest teaching Lala and Hermes have given me has been to value and love my body in the same way I value and love them. Just like Lala and Hermes, my body should not be ignored, abandoned, or mistreated. It should be paid attention to, fully claimed, protected, and profoundly cared for. It needs to play and rest, growl and stretch, eat yummy food, laugh out loud, and be around positive people. My body needs to be cherished and held and accepted as it is. It deserves to be wholly honored and wildly loved.

Now, years after Lala's adoption and my interview with Marion Woodman, I'm convinced that the most "spiritual" thing I can do is root my soul in my body, sink into this earth, and dare to truly *be here,* fully alive and completely in love.

While being embodied is an ongoing process and a daily practice, I'm lucky and grateful that two furry masters of embodiment live in my house, steal my food, lick my face, burrow in my bed, and curl or crash into me, continually reminding me:

You have a beloved body.
Be in it.
And remember, you are not so different from us.

ABOVE Cosmo and Sarah

Cosmo Perry Wiggins-Fernandez Soucy-Beasley

Sarah C. Beasley

Upon the death of my dog Cosmo, I placed a *takdrol*—a sacred Tibetan amulet enabling liberation upon touch—made by my teacher on the crown of his head. We performed a traditional Vajrayana Buddhist ceremony and *tsok* (feast) offering. Cosmo's body was left undisturbed for three days, as is traditionally done for human beings. The small, padded, tentlike structure he had inhabited in the last weeks of his life was draped with *khatas* (white silk scarves), and his puppy pictures were surrounded by candles, incense, and rose petals. His brown, black, gold, and white fur remained soft and vibrant, his ears perked up.

One afternoon, fifteen years earlier, I had driven to the animal shelter in Santa Fe to "just look around," having been warned by my partner that there was no such thing as browsing at the pound. He was unsure about us adopting a dog quite yet. I hadn't had one since my epileptic cocker spaniel died when I was twelve. I yearned for a dog who would share our mountain and desert adventures, and I fell for an aloof, four-month-old fuzzball who stuck to us like Velcro once we brought him home. I didn't know that within a year Cosmo would be my "transitional" creature as I moved away from the relationship. It broke my heart to leave my partner and our life together; outwardly it was all I wanted, but inwardly voices roared and whispered with turmoil and questions, and the knowledge that only a solitary path, for the time being, would enable me to begin unraveling internal disorder and confusion. I was drawn to search for a path and a wisdom teacher, although I scarcely knew it then. I had serious questions about death. I had to leave my cherished home behind to hunt for my own genuine heart. Years later, having come full circle, I would long for the outward connection of a loving home again. Having Cosmo with me during that search gave me the initial courage to leap, to trudge on, and to tune in authentically to my own shadows.

For eleven years, Cosmo was my steadfast companion. We lived in New Mexico and Austin, Texas, and we camped and explored all over Colorado, West Texas, Nevada, and the Sierras. A splendid sidekick in my blue Honda Civic, he stood poised on the folded-down back seat, inquisitive nose at my right shoulder. We went whitewater rafting, backpacking, swimming, and snowshoeing. We even rode up a ski lift to gawk at fall foliage in Santa Fe, which was one of Cosmo's more extreme experiences; he was power-shedding in terror! He adored mountain hikes, lake and ocean jaunts, rolling in snowbanks, or lounging on the couch with potato chips for a movie binge. Cosmo was born with a black belt in the Art of Nap. With Cosmo I felt adventurous, loved, and tended. I slept very safely, canine warmer on my feet.

Cosmo embodied the archetypes of confidante, protector, adventure partner, and muse. He didn't just love the games I proposed, he invented his own. Learning to find hidden objects by name and hiding things for me to find, he would bark and jump gleefully. Herding dogs can learn more than a hundred words in any language. Cosmo knew at least thirty, and we had a secret system of guttural noises, clicks, and gestures that meant a number of things like "Sit," "Look both ways," "Okay to cross." The "W" word was not uttered in vain around him; to suggest a walk but not follow through would be most unkind. He was a beautiful and beloved creature, even by admittedly non-dog people. Both on the road and out in the wilderness, Cosmo protected me from threat of wild animals or volatile humans on several crucial occasions. He was loyal, constant, affectionate, humorous, focused, playful, and had impeccable instincts for whom to trust or not. He was fastidious about his own grooming and was even teased for acting catlike! I'll admit, however, that on occasion he earned my temporary loathing by rolling in some foul, long-dead skunk or salmon.

While living in San Francisco, I was invited to join the traditional Vajrayana three-year retreat. By then I had been practicing Buddhism for five years. I was torn about giving up *all* aspects of worldly life, not yet knowing that pets would be prohibited. There had been dogs in previous groups, and I assumed Cosmo would be going into retreat with me. But my teacher changed the policy, based on his experience of a dog who died a slow and vocal death during a previous retreat. Vet care would be difficult at best in a remote mountain setting. The practical impediments were clear, but leaving Cosmo behind was heart-wrenching. I knew he might die while we were apart; I sobbed inconsolably the first three days in retreat. My constant companion since puppyhood, he was a twin spirit—my shadow and keeper. Yet Cosmo had many loving caretakers among my family and friends. On periodic retreat breaks I got to hear about his new adventures.

Although the journey is ultimately a solitary one, still the heart yearns for the companionship of one's familiars.

One lunchtime in retreat, I accidently brushed an insect off the picnic table and, afraid I had squished it, I instinctively cried, "Oh sorry!" Lama Tharchin Rinpoche, my root teacher, raised his hand as if to hit me and mimicked, "Oh sorry." It stunned me into understanding that a casual wish *to not cause harm* was insufficient. I must actively try to *prevent harm* and help beings. Because my teacher was rarely angered, his wrathful compassion remains a powerful and lasting lesson for me—one I value.

Lama Tharchin was my closest and most influential teacher, but he wasn't the first one to make a lasting impact on me. Three years before I adopted Cosmo, I met Taitetsu Unno, a leader in Buddhism's Pure Land School, who was teaching a Smith College course entitled Buddhist Thought. He invited us after hours to a local sitting meditation and to his house for Japanese tea ceremony, which he performed. I hadn't experienced anything like it—such masterful movements and gentle grace. I still remember the geometric, all-wood, sunken living area in which he performed the ceremony with precision, utmost attention, and love, while his little dog keenly observed. It struck me how Professor Unno related to his wife and to his dog (a shih tzu, I believe). He seemed to perceive these two figures in his familial mandala as pure beings. I had never seen someone approach an animal with reverence, with deep devotion.

That same year, my beloved sculpture professor and mentor Leonard DeLonga was dying from a brain tumor. One afternoon we, his teaching assistants, gathered around his wheelchair at his home to share companionship and questions about life and art. This was a tradition he had long upheld at the college cafeteria before our early-morning bronze castings. Though physically subdued, DeLonga's generosity and warmth beamed undiminished toward us and his wife, Sandy. I recall the stillness and his bright, impressionistic paintings covering the walls. Gently crying, DeLonga said, "I shed these tears because I love you." He was sorry for *our* sadness over him leaving us. He was the first bodhisattva I met, before I even knew the meaning of that word.

Dying may not be pretty, but it is natural. After my long retreat, I was reunited with an elderly Cosmo, and I cared for him in the last year of his life. He was given tramadol, an opioid painkiller, for his joint pain, and toward the end I administered morphine shots brought to me by caring mobile vets. I set up canine hospice care in my bedroom, with a doorway to the yard. My neighbor built a wooden ramp over the outside steps so Cosmo could be assisted in and out of the house more easily, and by the end he didn't leave his bed at all. One day, in exhausted frustration, I was helping him down the ramp to relieve himself outside and, near the bottom, I let go too soon. Cosmo fell off the end of the ramp. It was only a half-foot fall, but I was horrified. Among the few regrets I have (so far) in this lifetime, this one comes most often to mind when I am impatient with others' frailties or shortcomings. Of the ten-thousand tender times I cared for Cosmo, this one act of negligence was a heart-rending moment.

Since his death, many people have asked why I didn't euthanize my dog when he was so old and feeble—some view *not* euthanizing as cruel or sentimental. From the Buddhist perspective, however, the opposite is true. Lama Tharchin Rinpoche explained patiently, yet emphatically, that to end any being's life is a terrible act for them, as well as for us. Killing (including oneself) is forbidden for one who has taken refuge vows. If the karmic life stream is cut short intentionally, it must start over in a lesser or repeat path. The teachings of compassionate action are to let karma play out, suffering and all, to exhaust it. Our desire to reduce others' suffering is noble, and every effort is made to comfort the elderly and dying, short of euthanasia. Mingyur Rinpoche is quoted by multimedia artist Laurie Anderson in a *Fresh Air* radio interview (November 19, 2015) as saying: "Animals are like people. Animals approach death, then they back away, and you don't have the right to take that away from them. Be present for life, and for death if you can."

At the end of Cosmo's life, a friend remarked that my dog and I were so closely linked that perhaps he could not surrender into death. I had not slept a full night in quite some time because I was at his side doing mantra, prayers, singing to him, and stroking his head for hours each day. So I went to sleep in a separate room while she watched over my sweet creature. In the deep dark stillness of that night, Cosmo let go.

When I feel most downtrodden and alone, if I fall asleep with a broken-open heart, Cosmo appears in my dream as a puppy—playful, jubilant, beaming. He brought me so much joy, tenderness, and optimism, reminding me daily to tune in to my feelings and immediate needs, to prioritize smiling, laughing, and snuggling. I hope I can be as steady and graceful as my sweet pup in both life and dying. I pray to emulate my sublime teachers—Unno, DeLonga, Tsedrup Tharchin, Thinley Norbu, Anam Thubten—and many more precious examples who show the way of compassion, truth, and love. There are many deaths within one life, and to find one's true path requires renunciation of myriad outer attachments and reliance on one's innermost heart as compass. Although the journey is ultimately a solitary one, still the heart yearns for the companionship of one's familiars. I am grateful to my guides—canine and human and divine—who accompany me on this journey toward home. Especially those friends and lovers who have let me go, understanding my wildish searching nature would have it no other way, and knowing I would always circle back, loping in through the gate at dusk.

ABOVE Dodger and Susanna

The Tail of My Perfect Teacher

Susanna Weiss

t was late in the evening and the room was warm. Darkness filled the corners; I was drowsy. Suddenly, the teacher's words snapped my mind back from its drifting. I sat straight up on my meditation cushion as I heard, "In each moment of life, we are creating who we are." I was stunned by the realization that in even the most mundane, ordinary moments, the possibilities and opportunities were mine to choose. In every minute, I am steadily shaping what my life will look and feel like—indeed, who I will be. Every particle of time mattered, not just those spent studying, reading, and meditating.

It felt like a flash of *satori,* of comprehending the true nature of reality. I saw my existence as more spacious than I ever had before, as an ongoing opportunity to create either joy or sorrow. Just like Don Quixote in *Man of La Mancha,* I took a deep breath of life and considered how it should be lived. How would I do this? How could I possibly learn to handle this marvelous challenge? Did I need to find a guru? Unearth an obscure ancient text filled with scholarly philosophy?

That's when it occurred to me that I was already living with the perfect teacher. He was the most affectionate, nonjudging spiritual practitioner that I have ever known: the Artful Dodger. He was an exuberant, jubilant, people-loving golden retriever.

Dodger's passion for sharing love and unfailing good cheer was always evident. I was already his faithful student, fulfilling my role of simply being at the other end of the leash as he made his rounds of the neighborhood. One morning was especially poignant. As always, Dodger wanted to approach people sitting on a bench—they're at just the right "canine level" to receive his attention. That day he pulled toward two homeless men who sleep at the park's entrance. "Ah, you want to say good morning," I said as Dodger led me over to their bench.

My dog went to each man, and each smiled and petted him. And then he kissed them. He reached up to their faces and gave two or three little "kiss licks." They bent to accept them and smiled some more. My eyes filled with tears. Who kisses these homeless men and women? They may receive small gifts of charity from the few who don't pull away in aversion and fear, but who kisses them? My puppy dog, Dodger.

To accompany him as he trotted down the street was a privilege. It was heartwarming to witness his interactions with the children he was drawn to, or with the silent woman who sat for hours on end in the lobby of my building. Until Dodger gently laid his head upon her lap, I had never seen her smile. He would lead me along, greeting the people as they hurried to the subway. Without slowing down or even making physical contact, they seemed to reach out to "pet his aura," yet somehow they were changed by their encounter with Dodger.

There was a remarkable lesson to be learned from him as he pursued his métier. *He did it in complete silence.* Dodger listened, he watched, and he sniffed (which I don't necessarily recommend) and reminded me how frequently the best possible support is deep listening—being quiet and present for another. At the hospital where I did my chaplaincy I had an experience that taught me how true this is.

I'd managed to learn just enough Spanish to visit Latino patients and say, "*Buenas tardes. Me llamo Susanna. Yo hablo muy poco español.*" One woman eagerly clutched my hands and began a flood of Spanish that was incomprehensible to me. I said, "I'm so sorry, I don't understand. *No entiendo.*"

"*Sí, sí,*" the woman nodded, and she tightly held my hands as she spoke nonstop for at least ten minutes.

I could sense the pain and anguish that was pouring out of her, although I couldn't translate any of it. I sat silently and was present for her, accepting—without understanding the words—whatever she needed to say. As I left, she cried and kissed my hands and said over and over, "*Gracias, gracias.*"

She knew that I couldn't speak Spanish, but together we were able to share the language of humanity because I was willing to be a vessel, a listener to her story. Someone cared.

Dodger also had no requirements about the people with whom he interacted. They didn't need to look good or have proper manners. Dodger adored children. Any barefooted baby dangling from mom's chest in a Snugli was sure to get a thorough footbath and tickling if Dodger was allowed near. He was happy to receive ear pulls and awkward hits on the head from wobbling, gurgling toddlers. There was no judgment, no withholding of self until he was sure the person he was meeting was "okay." The spirit of lovingkindness within him was for everyone, no prerequisites. He was a true follower of Neem Karoli Baba's teaching, "Never put anyone out of your heart."

Despite his overwhelming energy and exuberance, Dodger had patience. He would plunk down on the street as he waited for someone he had spotted a block away and decided he'd like to meet. He waited with just the tip of his tail twitching back and forth as the person approached.

> Our courage to care for each other can be bolstered by the knowledge that we ourselves can be the most exquisite gift to someone.

Time and again, his persistence would win over the most reluctant stranger. Even the most curmudgeonly non-dog lover usually broke down, smiled, and said, "What a nice doggie!" The little tail twitch then turned into a big wag that pulled Dodger's entire back end from side to side.

This lesson of patience was valuable to me during my hospital rounds. Sometimes I'd be visiting a man not accustomed to expressing his feelings, and we'd chat about the deplorable food or the weather. Then I'd just sit and wait, open and quiet, ready to accept anything from him—this was my equivalent of Dodger's tail-tip twitching. And sometimes out of the silence would come sobs of fear, and the man would be able to speak his terror of pain, of dying.

Only because I used Dodger's method of calmly waiting did this even have a chance to happen. Without it, we would have shared a nice, cheerful, chaplaincy chat, then I'd have moved on to the next room, never allowing the space to honor the depths of what that man needed to express.

There are times when I've been inspired by Dodger's unwavering audacity and lack of ego. He had no need to save face or look good. If he was rejected by someone who recoiled with, "Ew, shoo, shoo!" he cheerfully backed off and moved on to the next possible recipient of his charm.

At times, we need that brashness. In the past, I would sometimes miss a chance to help a stranger because I was afraid to hurt their feelings. *They might be insulted by my offer to help. Who knows if they want it or even need it*? Now, for the most part, I've abandoned that delicacy. If I see someone who appears to be struggling, I offer to help in the most respectful and casual way I can. I've found that the rejections are few.

Enlisting Dodger's boldness certainly helped me when an elderly woman fell in the street. I went over and could see that she wasn't doing well. I feared she had suffered a small stroke. She repeatedly refused to go to the emergency room, but agreed to let me take her home where we would call her doctor.

There wasn't an available taxicab in sight, but there was a lot of competition for any that came along. As a rushing businessman with his power briefcase and cell phone snagged a cab near us, I called out, "Hey, you, we need that cab!" To my amazement, he meekly opened the door and waited for us as we staggered along the sidewalk.

When we arrived at the woman's building and tried to cross the street, I feared we were going down together. She was leaning so heavily and was so unsteady that I could no longer hold her up. "Help, quick!" I barked out to a big, tattooed guy wearing a leather jacket with chains who was walking along eating his lunch. He dropped his McDonald's bag, french fries flying, and rushed to lift us both onto our feet as if we weighed nothing. Unabashed chutzpah was the best practice that day.

Our courage to care for each other can be bolstered by the knowledge that we ourselves can be the most exquisite gift to someone. One day on Dodger's walk, I stopped to give some money to a homeless woman. She accepted it, but she really lit up when Dodger started making a fuss over her, jumping around, licking, and playing with her. "He likes me!" she said, her eyes shining. The generosity of sharing ourselves with another is indeed a worthy gift. A dollar is nice, but so often it cannot compare to kindness, offering care and our presence.

Then there is perhaps one of the most difficult tasks: giving to oneself. To forgive ourselves, to be truly present to all facets of our humanity, allows the best within us to flourish. It lights not only our own way through the darkness, but a path for the world.

In this task of ministering to self, Dodger was an expert. He would eagerly grab a piece of chicken off the kitchen counter in order to experience the pleasure of scarfing it down. Shamelessly sitting on someone's feet so they would take notice and pet him was always in his repertoire. He embraced both sides of the wisdom "The only true happiness in life is to love and be loved."

An ancient legend has it that after death we will meet all the animals we have ever encountered, and they will be the ones to judge us. Dodger will be ready to accept us as worthy.

ABOVE   Yogi (left), Tsem Rinpoche, Dharma, and Oser

Caring for Animals
as a Spiritual Practice

His Eminence the 25th Tsem Tulku Rinpoche

From a very young age, I have liked all types of animals, especially mammals and birds. I have kept whatever I actually could—hamsters, fish, rescued squirrels, birds, dogs, turtles—since I was a child. When I finally settled in Malaysia as an adult, I contemplated getting a dog. It took me some time to decide, because I do not see dogs as so-called pets, something merely to entertain me, keep me company, play with, or use to show off. For me, a dog is a family member, a responsibility for the rest of its life and mine.

I believe some animals like dogs *are* very aware, and each provides some kind of service or assistance for their caretakers. After all, there are many stories of animals saving lives or alerting people to the onset of epileptic attacks or even earthquakes. In general, however, I try not to approach animals with a me-centric attitude or the expectation that they can enhance my life by providing some kind of service.

For me, an animal is not something for me to keep; I do not think of them on the basis of what they will do for me. What I like to do is make sure they are free from pain, mental anxiety, and disease and that they live in a healthy environment. This means they have room to play and get fresh air. It also means that they have a chance to interact, to get attention, to receive a lot of love, and basically to be free from harm.

I feel whatever animal I bring home has some kind of karmic affinity for me, and I will open my heart and my home to them. Once they become a permanent member of my household, I will be very alert and careful, and I will always be vigilant about making sure they are safe, happy, and free from harm. So for me, I always think about what I can do for *them*.

Focusing Out

Having a dog in our lives can benefit our dharma practice because some people are not used to looking after the needs of others. Having a dog compels us to focus outward. It trains the caretaker to see what the dog needs, what they like, and what they are uncomfortable with. Because the dog cannot speak, the caretaker must be very alert to understand if the dog is in pain or in need of something. Having a dog really hones your senses to be more alert, to have that extra care, and to schedule yourself around that little individual, for example, if they are unwell or sick.

All of this can help us to develop Dharmically as a meditative practice. I believe it is an important practice to make your senses sharper and train your mind to focus outward on others and their needs. This involves developing the care to be alert and anticipate what others might require in the future and to do something for them *now*. In an ordinary, worldly environment, very caring parents can predict what their children will need or foresee some danger and will do something in the present so that when the time comes, their children can adjust easily. Similarly, when we have little animals around us, we need to foresee what they need and observe and "listen" to them. It may be harder with animals because animals cannot speak, so it becomes even more vital for us to attune ourselves to them, to know what they need to be comfortable, happy, and free from danger.

Caring for and watching over animals is very Dharmic because it opens up our senses. It opens our minds to focus outward more and to think harder and in greater detail about that individual's needs. Sensory-wise, when we watch over animals we must be sharper so that we can protect them and make sure they are okay, simply because they cannot talk. For me, having a dog is similar to dharma practice in the sense that it is focusing out as opposed to focusing in.

If we are to have pets, I believe in training them when they are very young because they are like human children; training them positively will result in happy adults or, in the case of animals, happy adult animals. If you neglect to train them when they are young, they might be difficult to manage when they are older. This is where some pet owners run into trouble—they think animals are there to entertain us, keep us company, and do our bidding. Some even project that animals can think like us, assume like us, and can put two and two together just like us. Perhaps some animals *can* do this, but pet owners should not generalize in this manner because it leads to having lots of expectations of what they want and need from the animal, and if these expectations are not fulfilled, they may feel the animal is not worth taking care of, keeping, or watching. That is wrong and unfair for the animal because in that case, we are not keeping it on the basis of it being an individual with the right to be happy, we are keeping it on the basis of "me, myself, and I" and what the animal does for us.

It is more about taking care of that individual who has the karma to be with me. That is one aspect of keeping animals around me. The other aspect is that I sincerely like animals.

> For me, having a dog is similar to dharma practice in the sense it is focusing out as opposed to focusing in.

Practicing Equanimity

My relationship with animals is like my relationship with people: I believe in treating them all equally. I get along with some people and I do not get along with others; I get along with some animals and I do not get along with others. Whether or not I get along with a person, however, does not preclude me from helping them. Similarly, whether or not I get along with an animal does not determine whether they deserve happiness, safety, food, and comfort. Hence, I do not treat animals on the basis of the way they treat me. I treat animals with kindness because I see them as having more suffering and difficulties, and less control of their lives. Because of this, I have a sort of sympathy—and for some animals, pity—that they suffer so much.

I do not like animals to suffer, to be cruelly treated, or to be harmed, beaten, or slaughtered in any way, for any purpose—whether it is to feed me, to entertain me (as in circuses), or to let out aggression. I do not believe that any individual should suffer at our expense. Animals should not suffer for our pleasure or our gratification because when they do, the pain they feel is equal to ours. Because they can feel pain and suffer physically, they can experience tremendous mental anguish. Why would we want to inflict that kind of experience on a little animal? Why would we want to inflict pain on an animal, or make them suffer, experience anxiety, torture, beatings, and slaughter?

Why would we want to do that? It does not make sense. If someone cuts us, it hurts; if someone pinches or hits us, it hurts; if someone abuses us mentally, it hurts. Similarly, if we pinch, cut, and abuse another individual, be it human or animal, it hurts them, too. As sentient beings, we should be aware of this pain they are experiencing and how unpleasant it is for them, just as it would be unpleasant for us. And if we feel pleasure in inflicting pain on others, it is not real pleasure but a distortion of the mind. To be aware of this, to refrain from hurting animals, and to do our best to protect and feed them is also a spiritual practice.

A Question of World Peace and Karma

Why is that a spiritual practice? Empathy, compassion, and care for sentient beings are all qualities of spirituality. Developing these qualities leads to spiritual development. All sentient beings deserve to be happy; all sentient beings deserve to be free from suffering and anxiety. Therefore, if we can create this type of atmosphere in our personal environment—in which beings are free from pain, hunger, and anxiety—why wouldn't we?

The more we do that for others, the more we will grow spiritually because the whole purpose of spiritual practice is the development of kindness. When the kind mind, the kind heart, the kind attitude, and the kind individual grows within our families, our neighborhoods, our towns, and our society, eventually—hopefully—the kindness becomes global. All of this can start with any sentient being, be it animal or human. Hence, when we are kind to beings all around us, we develop the kindness within us until it becomes spontaneous, natural, genuine, and real. Developing this kindness is spiritual practice and can be done relative to care, empathy, and compassion for animals.

Some people believe that when we die we will go to heaven or a pure land, or that we will take a good rebirth if we lived our lives well. Maybe that is the case; maybe it is not the case. But what is universal, recognizable, and crucial for us to understand is that the pain created for others creates an energy called karma that *does* return to us, and that *does* create pain.

Regardless of the level of being we have hurt—whether human or animal—the pain they experience creates karmic energy. When we create that energy it will come back to us, so as spiritual people our first awareness should be karma—how we create it, where it comes from, and how we can stop or redirect it.

One of the best ways we can stop this karma is by not inflicting any pain on other sentient beings. It is very easy to start with animals because they do nothing to harm us. They are vulnerable, weaker, and in some cases perhaps not as mentally evolved. Therefore, to hurt such a being who is not our so-called equal is not a fair fight. Likewise, it will not benefit us spiritually to harm animals, abuse our environment, or fail to provide proper care to the beings around us. This behavior contradicts the goal of spiritual practice, which is to develop a very kind heart and mind. A kind mind is a mind that is ready to assist others in any way, shape, or form by engaging in peaceful, wrathful, skillful, or comedic means. We do whatever it takes to help the other being.

Personally Speaking

The Buddha has taught that the real motivation for our practice is to benefit and liberate all sentient beings from suffering and *samsara,* and this teaching includes animals. I believe in liberating animals and being kind to every creature that I see, as best as I can. I feed animals everywhere I go; I keep animal food in my car at all times so that if I see a hungry animal I can stop the car and feed them. It makes me happy to know that for that day they have some food.

Taking care of animals and, in this case, taking care of dogs we call pets helps us develop awareness and kindness, and to focus outward. So taking care of pets is a spiritual journey and has been a spiritual practice for me. We need only understand that genuine dharma practice is about benefiting all of those around us, whether two- or four-legged, and to realize that spiritual practice can be engaged in at any time, anywhere, and with anyone. Ultimately, what do we really want? A kinder, more compassionate mind. Caring for animals and being alert to their needs can help us attain that.

Sometimes the Best Teacher
Is the One Who Made
You Cuss the Most

Joan Ranquet

once lived with the most perfect dog on the planet. Olivia was smart, funny, clever, energetic, flexible, healing, and inspiring. She was half border collie, one-quarter German shepherd, one-quarter rottweiler, and 100 percent Scorpio. We lived in Denver, South Florida, and then the Seattle area. We climbed several "Fourteeners," as they call them in the Rockies—peaks with an elevation over 14,000 feet. We loved to walk on the beach, and we raced through the woods of the Pacific Northwest.

But, this story isn't about Olivia, it is about Isabella, the other dog who walked into my life and claimed major real estate in my heart.

One day, my friend Linda called me. Linda has a kennel/boarding business and she runs a rescue dedicated to bully breeds and unadoptable dogs. She can turn an aggressive pit bull into a nanny for a screaming infant and a bouncing toddler faster than anyone I've ever seen. Linda wanted an animal-communication session for a rescued dog. In my vocation as an animal communicator, I am able to "talk to animals" or understand how they are feeling or thinking through telepathy, the transference of pictures, words, and feelings. Linda warned me that she might have to euthanize the dog

I was about to connect with because she was completely feral. When she said this, I knew it would be a challenging case.

For nearly a month, the dog Sarah was so frightened of people that she was fed at one end of an empty barn while her caretakers hid. Sarah skulked out, inhaled the food, and dashed back to her secret spot. Nobody could catch her; nobody could touch her. The rescue workers assessed that there must have been abuse to make the dog this sketchy.

Sarah had been found running on the street, pregnant, presumed to be about three years old. When she was brought into the Humane Society, they immediately spayed her, even though she was days away from delivery. Twelve puppies were aborted. Linda told me story after story that made Sarah's fear of people seemed insurmountable.

When I tuned in to Sarah, she fired off a series of telepathic stories; among many images, the most striking was that she was a dog who loved her family. She had been adored by a guy. She was too much dog for the wife caring for two babies. She had been a loveable, goofy, funny dog. Sarah was heartbroken, and somehow she was separated from her family. She ended up on the streets, surviving.

Linda was surprised to hear that there was love in the dog's past because Sarah seemed so street savvy. She had brought the dog to me for energy work in hopes of peeling away the layers that had shut down Sarah and of finding the dog who had once loved a family.

Before I hung up the phone with Linda, words tumbled out of my mouth that I had zero connection to: "If she gets along with Olivia, I could foster her." Because clearly, I didn't have enough going on in my life with the farm, the horse care, my work, my dying father, and a book coming out. Yes, let me just add fostering a feral dog to my plate. *Awesome choice, Joan!*

Linda had to drug Sarah in order to get her to my place. We brought Sarah into my living room. She was a black Lab, supermodel gorgeous. When dogs are that tenuous, I don't take it personally and I don't have to touch them to work on them. Yet she came over to me. Linda was stunned. Sarah laid down, ready for our session to begin.

Through the course of the energy work, I quieted her system by "running energy"—feeling into her whole body, sensing her chakras, and bringing in a high-frequency energy called the scalar wave. As I did this, Sarah melted and became one with the floor! As she relaxed, I could feel a layer of bracing, guarded energy lift from her. When I finished, Linda and I spoke for a few minutes. As Linda stood, Sarah shot up, raced to the bathroom, and hid. My dog Olivia didn't seem to mind Sarah, which meant I had a new dog to care for. Although I had no intention of keeping her, I changed her name to Isabella.

Love is everything.

Isabella took comfort in one of the many dog beds in the house. I figured if I ignored her and treated her like a feral cat she could at least feel safe enough to unwind a bit. Soon, a very loud, high-pitched sound startled me. I discovered that Isabella was crying in her sleep. Dog crying—no, actually dog wailing. This went on for some time. I couldn't touch her; that would betray the thin level of trust we had built. Plus, I didn't know if she was a biter. So, I held space for her to just cry it out.

When Isabella awoke, I told her that Olivia and I had experienced a lot of loss recently as well and that we would be joining her with our collective mourning for a grief fest.

About six hours into our foster experience, I sat down at my computer. Suddenly a dog was nuzzling at my lap. I stroked the head, assuming it was Olivia. When I got to the ears, they weren't pointy like Olivia's, they were super-soft Lab ears—little velvet angel wings.

I picked up the phone, called Linda, and requested immediate adoption. This feral dog was literally in my lap.

Lesson 1

If you give animals space to be who they are, they may become interested in engagement.
Or they are hungry.

All the little things I took for granted with a normal dog became obstacles over the next few months. How do I get a feral dog out the door? How do I get a screaming dog off her belly when I put a leash on her? How do I get her to pause her Cujo-style maniacal barking and listen to me when someone approaches the door?

I discovered early on that although Isabella wasn't going to necessarily do anything *I* asked, she learned a lot from Olivia. I don't know if she was learning for the first time or remembering how to be a good citizen, but Isabella had an awesome blank stare when I asked her to do things—except for one. If I asked her to "watch the video" she would look over at Olivia, and Olivia would demonstrate what I wanted Isabella to do, and then we were golden—Isabella would do it. She liked learning from Olivia better than me. Thankfully, Olivia was born to teach, and I didn't take it personally.

Lesson 2

Don't take animal behavior personally.

At that point, Olivia was a better pack leader. She was clear, she was neutral, she had an intention, she wasn't invested in a story, and she was not going to back down. She was what I have always referred to as an "emotional leader."

I blew through several dog trainers. Each told me that I had to consider the dog that was in front of me. I would say, "I am considering the dog. I want her to be at such ease in her body that she could be in the room like Olivia is when I teach!" Every single dog trainer shook their head as if I were a big dreamer.

I am a dreamer . . . *and* I knew people were coming to my house soon for an animal communication class. I couldn't have Isabella bolting through a window.

With all the things we overcame, my biggest challenge remained: when we all went out for nighttime barn chores and to tuck in the horses, Isabella often slipped into the dark, terrifying me, frustrating me, devastating me, and dumbfounding me that she could disappear so quickly. She could even vanish in the light of day—in the blink of an eye. I only had myself to blame. One minute she was there, the next minute she wasn't. I wasn't as fast as she was, so it was pointless to run into the black woods by myself. That's when I took up cussing.

Lesson 3

Cussing doesn't necessarily bring the dog back, but it sure feels good.

Like Maria racing back to the Abbey in *The Sound of Music,* Isabella would eventually rush back to me. As she galloped toward home, her velvet angel ears flapped like mad, trying to get lift-off and transport her over the distance to the front door. Upon her return she'd be completely conflicted: her sorrow for having done something wrong was rivaled by the pure glee of having had a free roam. Fundamentally, she didn't understand what was wrong about it.

Olivia never minded if another animal (dog, cat, or horse) misbehaved—it just elevated her status. She watched Isabella's struggle with complete superiority.

Every morning Isabella's enthusiasm for the day increased, only to be eclipsed by her extreme goofiness. There were so many beautiful, innocent discoveries as her grief subsided and acceptance settled in.

Isabella never met a garbage can she didn't love. You can take a girl off the streets, but you can't take the street out of the girl. If things were just a little too quiet, I could find her around the back of the house revisiting the week in garbage. Again, I had only myself to blame. Cussing was a great relief.

Lesson 4

Instinct lives on, no matter how much luxury you provide your animal companion.

The couch became Isabella's home base, her security. I allowed it because of her extreme anxiety. She injured herself repeatedly in a crate. The couch made her appear to be on perpetual holiday. Her slow arousal to do anything was the polar opposite of the temperament of my horses, Olivia, and me. (I am half border collie.) Isabella has an excellent guard bark . . . from the couch.

Olivia and I loved obedience, agility, and sheepherding. I couldn't train Isabella if my life depended on it. That blank stare became even more vacant when commands were uttered.

There were times when I could feel her connecting up with someone from her past, as if they each lamented their loss across the telepathic ethers. I knew I couldn't find the original owner. Body-work didn't have the desired impact of putting Isabella in her body. Energy work wasn't as potent as it often can be. Our love for her hadn't imprinted yet.

That's when I created Toy Parade—a celebration of nothing and everything, the perfect pattern interrupt to bring Isabella back into the present moment in joy. When I picked up a toy and yelled, "Toy Parade!" Isabella followed me and Olivia as we circled the furniture. This change always brought Isabella back into her body and a state of delight! Although Olivia thrived on her smarts and ability to run the farm better than I could, Isabella thrived on joy.

Lesson 5
Emotional intelligence is equal to book smarts.

Slowly but surely, the vision I had of a well-balanced, loveable dog who could be comfortable while I taught merged with the black dog who had moved into our house. From the first workshop on, Isabella remains the elegant, loving, quirky greeter at my workshops.

Equally, she loves large pack walks, visiting dogs—really, any guest species is welcome in Isabella's world! As new family members joined (cats, another horse, and another dog), she gracefully guided, babysat, nurtured, and protected them all in a single breath. She is the heart of the house.

That first six months was dog school for me. I became a better person for it, even through all of the cussing! I learned dog training with Olivia; I learned dog behavior with Isabella. I became an emotional leader, and we all rose to a new level of harmony.

I came to understand that Isabella's sketchy behavior wasn't the result of abuse, it was the shock of loss. Her love was so epic that on the streets she'd become an empty shell of a dog who could only spring back to life when her being was filled again with love.

Lesson 6

Love is everything.

ABOVE Chandi and Lama Surya

Dogitation:
Meditating with Chandi

Lama Surya Das

lived in Asia during my twenties and thirties. Refugee camps and monasteries are not always pet-friendly environments, so I didn't really become a dog person until I was in my forties. That's when I returned to the States and, thanks to my partner at the time, Chandi came into my life. She was a beautiful, white Hungarian sheepdog named for the Hindu moon goddess. Chandi broke my heart open to loving unconditionally rather than just loving to be loved.

I'm a dharma teacher; I work with students all the time, and I think the core teaching of Buddhism is to help people become less self-centered and learn how to give love to others. Chandi helped me along my bodhisattva path. She needed me and wasn't afraid to show it, and maybe I needed her and didn't have to show it, and this helped me grow. We were both vulnerable and permeable, and she melted my heart. When Chandi and I were together there was nothing missing; I didn't think about the future or the past—or even the present. She didn't care if I succeeded or failed, who I voted for, how much money I made, or whether I was enlightened or not.

In the mornings when I walked Chandi, that dog time became the best part of my day, what I came to call my *dogitation*. It was as fresh and innocent as nowness awareness, every morning for half an hour, an hour, or more. We met dog people along the way and often didn't know their names or what they did. Being with Chandi allowed me to just be like a true "person of no rank," as they say in Zen Buddhism: a dog-walking person with the other dog-walking people in the dog park picking up dog shit and carrying it home in little plastic bags.

I prayed and aspired to become the man Chandi thought I was. After our morning walk, I liked to sit down with her in my meditation room. "Sit," my mind said in Dog-Zen fashion—and my prayers were already answered. I was moved from seeing otherness to togetherness-oneness. While I gazed worshipfully at my Buddhist altar shrine—an old Buddha statue from Tibet and pictures of my gurus—my dog stared worshipfully at me. I was she, and she was me, and Buddha was we. We were all together, and all was well with the world, making me a jolly lama.

Here's a dogitation that we all can practice with a pet or a memory of a pet:

> Sit down with your animal friend. Assume the position.
> He or she might be on the floor in front of you, at your side, or on your lap,
> wherever is most comfortable and familiar.
> Be at ease together,
> attuned to each other in your familiar spiritual embrace.
> Start breathing together.
> Place one hand on your belly and the other on your dog's
> to help you stay grounded and sound.
> Let it happen, without
> obsessing about it, wondering whether you're properly
> synchronized or not. Dogs have no plans.
> In pet-time there's no time, no appointments
> and no disappointments.
> All good, the Primordial Time Zone.
> Let it all settle. Let go; let come and go;
> let be. If your dog is facing you, gaze into its eyes.

Relax, let the natural rhythms of dogitation
overtake you
and unite you both
in the space that only all animal lovers know.
Enter into the great timeless circle of cosmic breathing
with your silent accomplice
and pet-partner in co-meditation.

One time, my lama, Nyoshul Khenpo Rinpoche, and his wife came to visit me in Massachusetts. We spent a lot of time together in the car as I drove them to various teaching and ceremonial events. When I saw their faces in my rearview mirror I'd think, "This is wonderful! I'm serving the dharma. I'm with my master. I'm bringing him to my friends and students and fellows. My life has meaning!" A few weeks after he left, I was driving and Chandi was in the back seat of my car. She popped up over the seat, and I saw her face in the rearview mirror, her tongue hanging out, and I thought, "Holy crap! The absurdity of things. I'm driving Chandi around; my life has meaning!" It was a great "all beings equal before Buddha and God" moment.

> Chandi broke my heart open to loving unconditionally rather than just loving to be loved.

I'm not going to start a new religion of Dogism, but I am getting a little tired of religions and their limitations, prejudices, and biases, so it's important to think about what really opens our hearts or helps us be more authentic and free and less self-conscious and into strategic giving. There's a saying, "Dog is God spelled backward," to which I always add, "Scratch a dog and you'll find a God." Chandi and I belonged together, that's all I know. It wasn't a big decision; nobody needed to approve or agree. It's about the authentic relationship; it's not about the object or the subject. Who or whatever you co-meditate or meditate with, whatever you love, whatever opens your heart can be a real precipitant into the mystery and vastness of interbeing and oneness.

Meister Eckhart saw every creature as the Word of God. Who teaches and exemplifies that for us better than our own loyal pets, living in simplicity and delight, reveling enthusiastically in the senses as in eternity, while loving the one who feeds them? The sacred Buddhist Dhammapada teaches us that a master gives himself to whatever the moment brings. He doesn't think about his actions—they simply and naturally flow from the core of his being. Who better exemplifies this than a dog bounding after a ball or Frisbee? I love meeting different dogs on the street and inquiring into their being, their selves, and how they are so I can better care for them, just like people. You never know who you might meet, reincarnated in the form of that dog. Most of us overlook the immediacy and richness of experience right beneath our noses, but not a dog! The nose knows.

Dogs lead us back to a kinder and gentler, more nonverbal, joyous, trusting, and totally innocent, in-the-moment, childlike world—a sacred space of *this moment, only moment,* as the Mahamudra teaching puts it. Our dogs bow and say "bow-wow" to any and all comers, with impartial equanimity. When I no longer seem to know if I'm a man looking at a dog or a dog looking at a man, what worries could I have?

Chandi died a decade ago, but I still have a picture of her on my family altar. Love is the way, the truth, and the light—and everything else—so we all need to learn to love and be loved and let it in and out. Chandi helped me do that. My dog.

ABOVE Adyashanti

LEFT Kinte

The Dog of My Life

Adyashanti

The high mountains have always been my cathedral. They've been the place where my spirit soars; something quite wonderful happens throughout my whole being when I'm in them. There was a time in my twenties and early thirties when I did a lot of backpacking. I often went into the Sierra Nevada Mountains for two, three, or even four months in the summer, coming out only to get supplies. At one point, I decided it would be nice to do this with a dog, to have a companion, because I spent so much time out there by myself.

It seemed reasonable to find a dog that needed an owner, a dog somebody had rejected or had been found wandering. I went to the pound (now they call them animal shelters) and started looking at all the dogs. I was drawn to one in particular—a German shepherd and husky mix. Anyone who has had a pet knows how this goes. I studied the dog, and he had a certain gaze. Even though I could tell he wasn't happy about being there, I felt a spontaneous, intuitive connection with him, as if I recognized something in him just as he recognized that something in me. I patted him through the fence and talked to him to see how he responded. He took to me quickly. Then I read the little write-up the shelter had written about him, but it wasn't hopeful: the reasons his previous owners got rid of this dog were because he dug holes all over their backyard and he wasn't good with small children. Two qualities that you look for in dogs are that they aren't going to tear up your house by chewing everything and are going to be good around people, especially children. Despite this, I had a deep intuitive sense about the dog. I hung out with him for a while and decided to rely on my intuitive sense: I didn't know why this dog had caused those problems, but I had the feeling he was fantastic.

I took him home and named him Kinte. He ended up being the dog of my life. We grew very close. He followed me through the house; wherever I went, there he'd go. If I walked into a room and closed the door, he'd sit and wait for me. He'd ride in the car with me. He was so well behaved that I didn't have to put him on a leash. He turned out to be very gentle around children. I've never seen a dog or human being who had Kinte's patience with kids. They could do anything to him, and he'd let them. He never dug up our yard. Maybe it's because I exercised him a lot. He was a fantastic Frisbee player. He loved going out with me on ten- or fifteen-mile runs, and he loved to play and have fun. I took him backpacking, and he carried his own food and water in a side pack. We had some amazing experiences in the high mountains. Because of his breed—German shepherd and husky—he had great endurance and strength, and relished being out there; you could almost see a smile in the way that he parted his lips a little bit. He ended up being a wonderful, wonderful dog.

Kinte was my magical and beloved companion throughout my early twenties. Everyone who met him loved him because he loved people. He was active and yet kind and gentle and sensitive to people's feelings. He was one of those animals who is extraordinary at reading emotional energy—much more sensitive than most human beings. He had so many wonderful qualities, and we were extraordinarily close, which is why Kinte was my teacher in so many ways.

Humans like to share experiences, share life, share significant moments—and we can do this with pets. Not just the extraordinary times, but the everyday ones as well. Kinte taught me about forgiveness, about emotional attunement, sensitivity to others, about running *toward* in order to comfort people in difficulty—because that's what he did. He showed me that there's something intuitive about the emotional intelligence that many of us grow into as we get older, and our spiritual lives help with that emotional intelligence.

I loved Kinte and like to be around dogs in general because they simply are where they are; they feel what they feel. Everything is out in the open: they're not hiding anything; they're not protecting self-consciousness or a self-image like human beings often do. We love to relate, and yet we have to open up in order to relate.

Part of loving anything or anyone is having to say goodbye to them. Maybe they leave or you leave. The journey of loving begins by saying "hello" and welcoming something or someone into your life, and the journey ends with saying "goodbye" and letting a loved one exit. They may not exit your heart or your mind, but they're certainly going to depart—each one of us will.

Sadly, Kinte was no different. He developed a seizure disorder, a form of epilepsy that is common with German shepherds. I tried everything I could to treat him for it, but he had one seizure that went on for a long, long time and nothing we did could stop it. The vet said my dog had to be put down. It was devastating. I was overwhelmed with grief. I had lost my grandparents, who I'd been very close to, and other loved ones had died, but nothing struck me like the loss of this dog. I'd find myself in tears, sitting in the middle of the living room not knowing what to do. It seemed even more ridiculous because I was a twenty-five-year old guy, and I thought it odd that I would be so overwhelmingly struck with grief at the death of a dog. I had lost other dogs I'd grown up with and had always been sad when they left, but this was something of a different order. German shepherds tend to pick out one person to deeply bond with—it's like their lover for life—and we shared that profound relationship.

All true love sheds a tear.

My family had a little ceremony for Kinte in the backyard. We buried a few of his toys with him. I started to read the eulogy I'd written and the well of grief began to spill over—I could feel the sorrow coming. As I was reading, I decided to let go and allow myself to ride this profound wave of heartache that swept over me. Tears fell down my cheeks, over my chin, even onto the ground, and yet I kept reading.

That's when the strangest thing happened, perhaps because I'd completely let go to the experience of grief. Something unusual occurred right in the middle of my chest. It was as if a pinprick of light glowed from my sternum. As I continued to read and grieve fully, this pinprick of light grew bigger and bigger and bigger and bigger and bigger and bigger and went beyond my body, filling the space all around me. This light radiated a feeling of profound well-being—extraordinary happiness, contentment. It was my first deeply nondual emotional experience in the sense that it included both grief and happiness. It was the first time I realized that two completely opposing emotional states or states of being could simultaneously exist in the exact same space without any contradiction whatsoever, that in the core of my grief I could discover a profound sense of joy, contentment, peace, and well-being. One didn't overshadow the other—when the pinprick of light and well-being showed up, it didn't sweep away all the grief, it happened *in the midst of the grief*. The grief wasn't getting in the way of the joy, and the joy wasn't getting in the way of the grief; they existed as one totality, one gestalt, one moment.

I had faced grief and happiness before, but never simultaneously. Kinte's death marked the opening of a whole new dimension of understanding for me. I came to see as years went on that any deeply negative emotion that we completely open ourselves to will have a way of showing its opposite. I think of it now like looking at a coin—on one side it's heads, on the other side it's tails, but it's the same coin. Grief and peace aren't actually separate—they exist as one complete entity. I experienced this whole, this unifying of contrasting emotional experiences, because I completely and absolutely let go in the midst of a difficult experience.

As time went on, I realized that if we can get deep enough into an experience, it almost always includes its opposite. It's one thing to read about it, but it's something else entirely to practice it. When we do, it's liberating because we realize that even negative emotions can contain something extraordinarily positive. The nature of things is that everything arises as a simultaneity—like a package. We might see it as a package of duality—negative and positive. We can't necessarily find the light within darkness unless we completely surrender to the darkness, but then *the light can show up*. It's the same thing with positive experiences. One of my teachers used to say, "All true love sheds a tear," and we know when we experience the most profound love that there's something bittersweet about it—it's not all sweet. The deepest encounters with love include a bitter quality. Have you ever loved so intensely that it almost hurt to love that much? That's more in the range of what I'm talking about.

This coexistence of opposites is the true nature of human emotion and experience. It is an immense gestalt, although we usually recognize only joy *or* sadness, only grief *or* contentment, separate from the other. This happens for two reasons: One is that we are obsessively focused on the emotion we're experiencing, but we're not totally surrendered to it or we haven't completely let go. The other is that we're trying to contain and control at the same time that we're obsessing. When we do that, we only face one side, one aspect of the spectrum, or one side of the duality.

There are times when we undergo something deep and profound and something in us stops resisting, stops pushing against it, stops trying to contain whatever it is we're experiencing. When we can do that and not fall into indulging (starting to think about thoughts that make us feel worse), we can be with pure experience. There is no thought content, there is no storytelling going on one way or the other; it is an absolute openness to what is or whatever was in that moment. This was my dog Kinte's last gift to me. Even though I know the realization was coming from within myself, we had such a profound connection that it makes sense that his passing would in some way embody the profundity of our connection.

I felt called to share this story of my wonderful and beloved companion because that's what he was: more than a pet. And like any good companion, it's a journey, because you take care of each other. I did a lot to take care of Kinte, but he did as much to take care of me, and I'll never forget that lesson and that last gift I received while reading his eulogy in the backyard of my parents' house. As difficult as it was, I encountered a profound grace when I realized that the heart of our experiences is more multilayered and deep than we often imagine. Loving and saying goodbye to Kinte was a lesson about letting go. I don't mean letting go of something in order to get rid of it. When I let go *into* grief, profound joy showed up and the grief and the joy existed simultaneously. When we encounter the immensity of our own experience, we learn that it's so vast—it's not what it appears to be on the surface. There are multilayered, multitextured aspects of our experiences if we open deeply and profoundly to them and trust them—a lot of it comes down to trust.

No matter what or who you love—and by "love" I don't mean are entertained by or like, but rather what or who you *love* and give yourself to—it's expressed in that beautiful dance of giving and receiving in which the more you give, the more you receive, and the more you receive, the more you give. So it goes with humans and with pets—with me and with Kinte. Every part of our experience follows this profound way of unfolding.

LEFT   Zuijin and Roshi Joan

TOP RIGHT   Dogen and Roshi Joan

BOTTOM RIGHT   Dominga

And Yet, Dogs Find Me

Roshi Joan Halifax

often say that the most undefended relationship is with our dogs. I think my parents knew this intuitively, and so when I was recovering from a severe childhood illness, they introduced me to my first dog, Tiny Terence the Terrible. I think I named him that because he was a terrier and a bit of a barker. For short, I called him Terry.

Being with a totally affectionate and loyal creature stirred and overtook my heart, and I realized as a little girl that I was a dog person. Terry taught me many things, including how to love and how to grieve. My connection with him was more powerful than I was aware of.

One day, my mother told me that Terry had been poisoned by a neighbor. I sobbed uncontrollably. I could not fathom why someone would kill my dog. What kind of world was I living in if something like this could happen? It was my first taste of loss and death, and it being the result of human cruelty made it hard for me to reconcile.

My next dog was Chelsea. I was in my thirties when she came into my life. She was a foundling, discovered by an old friend who encountered this small, hungry, frightened German shepherd near the Chelsea Hotel in New York City. At the time, I was living at the Ojai Foundation in the Upper Ojai Valley in California. My friend thought I should have the dog. I assented, with reservations. He flew Chelsea to California.

Into my life came the most marvelous being—smart, small for a shepherd, affectionate, loyal, full of appreciation for having found a new life. Chelsea and I bonded and stayed together for years. She had the gift of sitting quietly for hours during meditation practice or when my community was meeting in council, as though she were part of our pack. I actually think we were *her* pack, as she roamed across The Ojai Foundation land with a sense of pride and ownership, visiting one resident after another, making her way back to my dwelling in the late evening to curl up next to me until dawn.

Chelsea was a gorgeous, deeply attuned being and my best friend, as dogs are wont to be. We were a duo, a pair. Years into our relationship I began to travel, and so I shared her with one of my students. It was difficult to let her go, but this student loved her, and I trusted that the next phase of Chelsea's life would be good. It was, but I always felt a sense of regret, a kind of hole in my heart that I was not with her in her final days.

Many years passed without a dog. I was traveling all over the world and could ill afford to have another canine friend in my life. One winter, I went to Tres Piedras in New Mexico to cross-country ski with friends. Ken, who was living in the "pink school house," was part of our ski gang. His dog, Hey Girl, had birthed a litter the month before, and Ken was convinced that one of the pups was mine. Being a Zen person, I was offered the black puppy; instead, the runt of the litter—the littlest one, with a deformed tail—captured my heart. I brought her home to the Upaya Zen Center, cupped in my hands.

I named her Dominga, as I had met her great-great-grandmother in Chiapas many years before. Dominga, the Elder, was a Mexican street dog and the beginning of a long line of dogs with the "Hey" name: Hey Girl, Hey Boy, Hey Man, and more. Instead of a "Hey" name, I chose her original ancestor's name, Dominga, meaning "Sunday."

For sixteen years, she was my closest buddy. For our first years together, we lived at Upaya Zen Center in Santa Fe, which I had founded. Fiercely protective, funny, independent, intimate, and (if she trusted you) loving. However, Dominga was also a menace to anyone who got near me and whose demeanor was even slightly assertive or aggressive. Too often I had to pull her off the leg of some unsuspecting person who ventured too close to me. As a result of this habit of attacking strangers, they hit, pepper-sprayed, and shouted at her, but she would not desist from protecting me. Finally, I moved with her to Prajna Mountain Forest Refuge so she could roam free and not scare the innocents who came to Upaya.

This is *kalyanamitra*— spiritual friendship at its best.

In her fifteenth year, Dominga began to slow down. Then, her legs could no longer carry her. My student Maria, who loved her, saw Dominga through six months of her dying. It was a tough journey for Maria, Dominga, and me. I was coming and going in my travels, and Dominga was growing more and more helpless. Maria's care and devotion were extraordinary, carrying Dominga out of the Upaya House to do her business, sleeping with her, and loving her when she cried in fear and confusion. Finally, the two of us sat with my old dog as she was released from this long siege of suffering.

Since Dominga, I have not had the heart to bring another dog into my life. I am a dog person, but I travel too much to bring another canine into my heart. And yet, dogs find me.

One year, after a hospitalization, I returned to Upaya to recover, and on my first evening home a monsoon hit Santa Fe. At midnight, I began to worry that our temple would be flooded again. Our senior residents were not around, and I did not know if there had been storm training for those who were on campus. The temple had been flooded twice by storms like this one, so I decided that it would be the wisest choice if I made my way across the property to check the storm drains.

It was after midnight, and the winds were high and the rain steep. I put on my bathrobe, went downstairs in the dark, and opened the front door, only to see a ghostly figure pass quickly in front of the Upaya House gate. I thought it might be a coyote, and was hesitant to proceed, but my worries about flooding pushed me into the night.

Halfway to the temple, something wrapped itself around my legs. I jumped, and then reached down to discover a large, thin dog shivering and clinging to me. I knelt and saw it was an old whippet. I hugged her and then urged her to follow me into River House, where I dried her off, got her some cheese from the fridge, sat on the floor next to her, and reassured her that she would be safe.

After about fifteen minutes, I asked her to accompany me to the temple, where I checked the drains and saw that all was okay enough. I then invited the dog to accompany me back to the Upaya House. I laid out my bathrobe on the floor next to my bed so she would have a comfortable place to sleep. She curled up in the green corduroy for all of a minute and then stretched her long body and slid onto my bed and into my arms. We both fell asleep until dawn.

I named her Zuijin—water spirit.

The next morning, I made my way to the temple for a final council of a program that was concluding at Upaya. Zuijin followed me to the Zendo and entered unselfconsciously into this beautiful place of practice. Our head priest, Genzan, made a weak protest when Zuijin walked the circle of people on their cushions and returned to settle onto a zabuton next to me.

The council was already in process when the temple doors swung open and a man burst into our midst, shouting, "Has anyone seen Roy?"

Roy? Who is Roy?

As it turned out, Roy was his dog, the whippet, my Zuijin! And Roy was a male and wasn't moving. It was a standoff between Roy and his owner, with me in between. There was no real choice—Roy had to go. He went very reluctantly, his owner pulling him by the collar out of the Zendo.

Zuijin, however, continues to visit Upaya, drifting like an old cloud through the temple grounds. He occasionally finds his way into the Zendo. Sometimes we are sitting and hear the tap-tap of his long, old toenails on the wooden floor. When this happens, I say to myself, "Well, this old monk is returning to his practice." I smile quietly.

I know the innocent grief from loss of a dog: Terry, Chelsea, Dominga. I also know the joy that can be found in relationship with one. I doubt the Buddha had a dog, but plenty of my Buddhist friends do. It is not hard to imagine why. For some of us, this is *kalyanamitra*—spiritual friendship at its best.

ABOVE Fenton and Pam

Mother's Day Storm

Pam Houston

I lost Fenton Johnson the wolfhound in May—Mother's Day weekend was his last—which, I know from experience, will make all the Mays from now on a little sadder.

Eleven years is a big number for an Irish wolfhound, and Fenton had made excellent use of every one. I named him after my dear friend, the writer Fenton Johnson, and as Fenton the dog grew up, he revealed more and more ways the name was apt. Like Fenton the human, he was wise and reticent like the best kind of grandfather, even when he was only middle aged. He wasn't big on asking for affection, wouldn't wiggle up to you like a black Lab or a Bernese mountain dog, wouldn't even very often bump his head up under your resting arm for a pet. He preferred to sit nearby, keeping a loving and watchful and ever-so-slightly-skeptical eye, as if the humans were always potentially on the verge of making a really bad decision, and he would be ready, in that case, to quietly intervene.

When Fenton was a young dog, he would bound through deep snow with an expression of such pure joy on his face it could make even a non-dog person laugh out loud. He would drink water only out of the very edge of a bowl, and only then with his top teeth pressing firmly against the metal rim. When he wanted something, he would come over and scratch on the chair or the couch I was sitting on, as if it were the wrong side of a door, as if to underscore his point that humans are often too stupid to interpret the telepathy and body language dogs so take for granted, and he would once again do his best to help us out. When he was happy—for instance, if I rose from a chair with a leash in my hand—he would wag his tail heartily; but when he was ecstatic—like when I came home after

133

a week of working on the road—his tail would make huge, happy circles, the scope of his happiness too big to be contained in a movement that only went from side to side.

To say that Fenton was intelligent, to say that he had a wider range of emotions than anyone I dated in my twenties and thirties, is really to only scratch the surface of what a magnificent creature he was. He was the ranch manager, hypervigilant but not neurotic, who kept his eye on everything—animals, people—making sure no one was out of sorts or out of place. Because of his watchfulness, he had perfected the art of anticipating what would happen next better than any person could have. He knew all of my tastes and my tendencies, and he was always ready to be of service in any undertaking: moving the sheep from one pasture to another, walking the fence line to look for breaks, riding into town to drop off the recycling, cheering me up on a sleepless night by resting his heavy head across one of my ankles, reminding me to get up from the computer after too many hours of writing and go take a walk outside.

His last year, though, the arthritis that first made itself known when he was about eight years old was getting severe. He'd been on Rimadyl—the doggie version of Advil—for a few years. We'd had good results from acupuncture, massage, glucosamine chondroitin, and most recently with laser treatments. Doc Howard had shelved his country-vet skepticism to give the laser gun a try and had been surprisingly impressed with the results, using it on many patients for pain relief, as well as on his wife and himself. And so once a week I loaded Fenton into the SUV and we drove to Doc's, donned our Keith Richards goggles (Fenton got some too), and Doc's granddaughter gave Fenton six shots of laser light in his back end. Eventually, even the laser gun treatments reached the point of diminishing returns.

I'd been away for a few days in Boston when I got the call from my house-sitter Kelly that Fenton was down and didn't seem to want to get up anymore. A wolfhound isn't meant to be unable to stand or walk around, however comfortable we might be willing to make him.

Months before, I had written on my calendar the following words: "This weekend keep free in case Fenton . . . ," and there was the old boy, as obliging as ever, doing everything, even dying, right on time. I flew to Denver immediately and invited some of Fenton's closest friends to the ranch for the weekend, knowing that in order to come, they would have to brave the predicted Mother's Day blizzard on the five-hour drive from the Front Range to the ranch.

In Boulder, at the Whole Foods, I bought dry-aged, organic beefsteaks for everyone I thought might make it, plus a mountain of other groceries, because I figured if we were going to be sad—and we *were* going to be sad—at least we would have good food to eat. When I selected the steaks, the Whole Foods butcher, whose name is Jerry (and whose dog's name, I would learn later, is Gristle), took a lot of time and great pleasure describing the dry-aging process. When I asked for six T-bones, one for each of the potential guests and another for the old boy himself, Jerry said, "You must be having quite a party." Because he had been so kind and thorough in *his* explanation, I said, "Well, what I am actually doing is having a kind of living wake for one of the best dogs who has ever lived, and I want to buy the very best for him and for his friends who are making the drive up to my ranch in Creede to be with him."

Jerry lifted one of the massive T-bones off the top of the pile that was sitting on the scale. "You should have said so to begin with. In that case, Fenton's is on me."

My friend Tami Anderson had a wonderful dog named Taylor who she was as deeply connected to, I believe, as I was connected to Fenton. I have loved all my dogs, of course, but there is the rare dog—I have had two so far in my life—that asked me to transcend my human limitations and be, at least occasionally, a little more evolved, like them. Fenton was such a dog, and so was Taylor. Taylor and Fenton were puppies together, and they loved each other truly all their lives. When Taylor was coming close to the end, she and Tami would often lie on the bed together and look into one another's eyes. One day, Tami told me, almost in a whisper, they were in such a position, and Tami said, "Maybe next time, I'll be the dog." And that is everything I will ever have to say about why I am friends with Tami.

Tami couldn't be there for Fenton's weekend, and neither could my partner, Greg, so it turned out to be me and Kelly and another house-sitter, Linda, who had cared for Fenton so often over the last five years of his life that he belonged to her nearly as much as he belonged to me. Linda had flown in from Reno and met me at the Denver airport, and we had driven up together, but everyone else who had wanted to be there had been kept away by the storm.

The weekend was everything all at once. It rained and snowed and blew and eventually howled, and I slept out on the dog porch with Fenton anyway, nose to nose with him for his last three nights. The storm seemed to have been ordered especially for the old boy, who loved the cold and snow most of all, who hated the wood stove and preferred it when we kept the house in the fifty-five-to sixty-degree range, who all his life would raise a disapproving eyebrow at me the moment he suspected I was going out to chop kindling.

Linda and I gave him sponge baths and rubbed his face and ears until he didn't want us to rub his face and ears anymore, and then we sat quietly beside him. I will admit to even loving cleaning him up, changing his dog beds, washing and drying him, fine-tuning my attention to meet his every need.

When I could stand to tear myself away from him, I cooked giant pots of soup and pesto and grilled vegetables and salad. I had no appetite, but the kitchen was warm and smelled good whenever I walked into it. Fenton ate Jerry's giant, dry-aged T-bone in three sittings over two days, and he enjoyed the bone as much as I'd ever seen him enjoy anything in his life, even though he'd mostly lost interest in other food by then. There were times I was sure we were doing exactly the right thing by Fenton, times I thought that if *my* last weekend could be like his, it would be better than pretty much anybody's last weekend I had heard about in the history of the world. Other times, I was in a flat panic. How could I be trusted to make this decision? What on earth gave me the authority or the wisdom to decide when the quality of life had crossed over some determinate line? And all that aside, how would I live in a world without him, without his tender presence beside me, without his increasingly stiff rear end galumphing down the driveway to meet me, without his quiet vigilance as I sat in a chair and did my work?

Fenton was my seventh Irish wolfhound and my tenth dog overall; I was not new to being the decision maker, but no amount of times down this difficult road seemed to make it any easier. At one point I got myself so freaked out I thought maybe we would get in the car together—just him and me—and drive and drive to see if we could outrun death.

On Monday morning I saw that he was getting the very beginnings of tiny sores from sitting still for so long, and I knew that Tuesday morning would have to be his last. My friend Kae called from Denver and said she had tried to make it on Sunday, but because of black ice they had closed Highway 285, and so far it had not reopened. She asked me if I was okay, and I told her that I was. I have always called Kae the moral center of my large and wonderful group of women friends, in part because she was raised by preachers, in part because she has so much backbone, but mostly because she has a remarkable way of orienting toward true north.

> Who in your life has ever been ecstatic over your arrival? Someone, I hope— some living being.

Kae and I have the same exact Prius—year and model—and when she pulled in the driveway ten hours later, Fenton got more excited than I had seen him all weekend—even though I was sitting right there beside him—like there might be two of me and that I might come home all over again and start caring for him as I already was. It was another unexpected gift of the weekend. How many hundreds of times had I seen Fenton at the bottom of the driveway, his tail going in giant crazy circles? But because I was always the one *in* the Prius I had never before witnessed that moment of recognition, the moment he became sure that *that* car *was* my car. Who in your life has ever been that ecstatic over your arrival? Someone, I hope—some living being.

Of course, it was not a second me who got out of the Prius, it was Kae, and when Fenton recognized her, he danced and danced on his front legs only, because he loves her, too, and he knew she had come to see him. As a culture, whenever we want to treat someone or something inhumanely, we declare that they don't have emotions, but anyone who thinks dogs don't have emotions should have been on the porch that night in the snow.

Kae had driven ten hours in white-out conditions, which doubled the length of the drive. When I asked her if it was awful, she shrugged and said, "You never *ever* ask for help, so after we talked, I figured I needed to get here."

I said, "I don't think I asked for help this time."

"Maybe not. But you were close."

We bedded down on the dog porch in sleeping bags under the swirling snow. She said, "You are doing the right thing, Pam; he's not going to get better."

"It feels like a betrayal no matter what I do."

And she said, "I don't think *betrayal* is a word that belongs on this porch."

I teach sometimes with the Colorado writer Laura Hendrie, and she gives a craft lecture on something she calls the Jaws-of-Life character, the person who sweeps in and pulls your protagonist from the burning car just when it seems that all hope is lost. Kae Penner-Howell was my Jaws-of-Life character that weekend. She came just when all my intrinsic strength and broadminded philosophy about the cycle of life was about to fail me. She drove ten hours in a Prius on black ice to sleep on a hard, wooden porch in a poorly rated sleeping bag with me and Fenton on his last night on earth.

I didn't want to go to sleep because the hours were short now and I didn't want to miss a minute. After we had been quiet for a while, a coyote barked and another howled back to him from a greater distance. Before long, and for the last time, Fenton joined their song.

A few hours later, when it was barely getting light, I lay nose to nose with him and petted his perfect ears and said, out loud, "You did such a good job, Fenton. You did such a good job taking care of me." He looked right at me, right into me. He wanted me to know he knew what I was saying.

"And I think you already know this," I said, "but you don't have to be afraid." I didn't know where those words came from—if it were me getting the shot in the morning, I sure as hell would be afraid—but I knew when I said them that they were the most important ones. In the gathering light, Fenton looked into my eyes not with fear exactly, but with urgency. He said, *Now it is my turn to trust you,* and I said, *You can.*

An owl hooted, some geese honked, and Kae stirred in her sleeping bag. One of the lambs started baa-ing—Queeny, probably, the one with the higher voice. I heard Roany nicker softly, heard him walk around on the crunching snow. Somewhere in the distance, the sound of a woodpecker. All the sounds the ranch makes every morning.

Doc Howard arrived at ten o'clock, through the snow, to give Fenton the shot. Doc is getting older, and he'd told me he would be sending his granddaughter in his place. I hadn't protested, though I knew he heard the disappointment and fear in my silence, so I was unsurprised and so very grateful to see his small, gray head behind the wheel. When I noticed that he did not have the sedative that most vets give initially—before they give the drug that stops the heart—he again heard my unasked question. Doc answered, "What's in this syringe is the world's biggest sedative; I don't like to mess around with lots of reactive drugs."

Fenton was calm—almost smiling—for the very few minutes it took to put him to sleep forever. I believe that he knew what was happening. I believe he was ready to put his head down on my lap one last time.

Everybody cried, even sweet Jay, Doc's brand-new vet tech who had only met Fenton a couple times. When I found my voice again, I told Doc the story about Jerry and the steaks, and he said, "Pam, it turns out there are a lot of really good people in the world."

After we loaded Fenton's body in Doc's truck to be taken to the morgue for cremation, Kae and Linda and I took a pasture walk in his honor. A couple of inches of snow covered the ground, and the Rocky Mountain bluebirds who had returned recently, hoping for better weather, were almost too beautiful to bear against the freshly whitened pasture. The sun came out, and we fed all the equines apples and carrots out of our hands.

Eight hours later I found myself back in the Denver airport, which was full of opportunities to do all the things I hadn't found the time or the wherewithal to do all weekend: drink water, go to the bathroom, eat food. My plane was delayed two hours, and the corn chowder at Elway's Bar tasted miraculous. I was riding on something I recognized as "having lived through the thing you thought you might not live through" adrenaline. I marveled at all the people around me who weren't grieving, who had had a normal weekend with their families at home. I wasn't sleepy exactly; it was more like the insides of my eyes had been scoured out with steel wool. Fenton the human sent me a text that said Fenton the canine loved and was loved all his life, and that there is no condition in all our living and dying that could be more satisfying than that. Months later he would write Fenton a eulogy that quoted both Thomas Merton (*What we have to be is what we are*) and Whitman (*Life is the little left over from the dying*), and in which he said, "Fenton the canine was a teacher . . . he taught through the simple fact of being who he is, who he was . . . In the losses lie the lessons . . . If we would only embrace death as another aspect of life—if we would let the animals teach us how to live and how to die—we might just treat each other and our animals better than we do."

As I waited for my plane, I found myself thinking back, as I had many times that weekend, to Jerry at the Whole Foods pulling that steak off the top of the pile. He might have thought what he did was a small thing—though the price of those dry-aged steaks makes it at least a medium thing, even by the most objective measure—but the relative magnitude of his kindness to me, at that moment, was frankly immeasurable, and I held onto it all weekend and for the weeks of grief to come.

Dodger and Allan

Golden Tails

Allan Lokos

There was no talk of feelings when I was growing up, so it is not surprising that as a young man my emotional life was muddled within my delicate, unenlightened psyche. Typically, and unknowingly, I converted suffering and sadness into anger and impatience. Since there was an abundance of suffering in my childhood, it was not surprising that I developed into an angry young man. Anger can be seductive because it has energy and juice—we can lash out and "get even." Conversely, hurt and sadness just feel bad and often leave us with a sense of helplessness.

It could have been anticipated then, that at the time of my divorce, instead of feeling the loss and grief that were present, I felt turmoil and anger—intensely pervasive and ongoing. Feeding that confluence of emotions was the fact that my little daughter Samantha had become, and would forever be, the child of a broken home. I was devastated and, consequently, more angry.

I was still several years away from encountering the dharma. So as one might expect, I looked for something outside of myself for solace and for healing the deep rift between my daughter and me. That something turned out to be an eight-week-old, unbelievably adorable, golden retriever whom Samantha immediately dubbed Beau. He was off-the-charts cute and unashamedly, indiscriminately, boundlessly loving. Food was his number-one passion, with people coming in a close second. He adored Samantha and had an abundance of affection for me as well. He loved rain and snow, peeing and pooping, trees and fire hydrants, and anything else worth sniffing—which was essentially everything.

This amazing ball of golden fuzz brought with him a tremendous potential for my healing process to begin. Unfortunately, I was too attached to anger, distress, and despair to accept his many gifts. Instead, he became the recipient of that anger and distress. These were among the darkest days of my life, and my behavior toward Beau was horrible. For years I believed there would be no way to ever forgive myself. No, I didn't beat him, or starve him, or neglect his daily needs, but I certainly wasn't his friend. I couldn't love him or anyone else, although I tried with Samantha.

Beau grew from an adorable puppy to a magnificent adult dog, but still he received little but scorn from me. I hardly noticed that while I was often obnoxious toward him, he was never anything but loving. Later, I began to wonder if in a previous life Beau had been an adept of the Brahma Viharas—the Four Immeasurables, or sublime states of lovingkindness, compassion, harmonious joy, and equanimity. These qualities of mind are incompatible with anger or hatefulness.

One day, I realized that, unlike many dogs, Beau liked being brushed—one of the few things we did together. He not only liked it, he knew exactly what to do during the routine. When I picked up the brush and sat on the floor, he came running from wherever he was and sat directly in front of me. I brushed one of his ears, and when I finished, he turned his head so I could brush the other. I then brushed his luxuriant ruff, and upon completion, without a word or gesture from me, he turned and presented me with his back. He then lay down on his back, paws dangling in the air, so I could brush his belly and finally his long, feathery tail. He would then get up quickly and again sit directly in front of me with his face radiating enormous pride. (Okay, I'm anthropomorphizing a bit.)

Beau was irresistible. I had to grab him and hug him, and he would lick my face in kind. Perhaps that is how it began—Beau's teaching me the dharma: just because the other person is a jerk doesn't mean you have to be. Be consistent with your loving friendliness and compassion. Maintain your equanimity. Beau had his act together and he never quit on me. I'm not sure exactly when it happened, but Beau's consistent, boundless love got through to me and a transformation began.

It happens that the Buddhadharma (as differentiated from the *Beaudharma)* entered my life at about that time, as did another wise and beautiful being. Susanna and I married a few months later, and I wasn't the only one deeply in love with her. I learned that golden retrievers are extremely loyal—to the next person. Beau couldn't get enough of Susanna and vice versa. Beau had taught me well, however, and instead of feeling envy, I rejoiced in their happiness. *Mudita*, which I like to translate as "harmonious joy" (others prefer "sympathetic" or "appreciative" joy), is rejoicing in the happiness and good fortune of others. It flowed easily as these two beautiful beings reveled in each other's company. (After a routine visit to the veterinarian, the doctor asked if a new female canine had come into Beau's life. He had found an excessive amount of semen in the dog's urine. Our shy vet blushed when we identified Beau's new romantic interest.)

> In any given moment, we are all doing the best we can.

Beau did his best to teach me about forgiveness. He certainly was an exemplar. During that difficult period of my life when I was such a poor companion to him, he shook off my faults and came back again and again with unbounded love. Yet, I could never forgive myself, even years after he died. How could someone be mean to a golden retriever puppy? It seemed inhuman; my actions were unforgivable. I secretly carried the burden for years, feeling that anyone who knew this truth would surely despise me.

One evening I was teaching a workshop that focused on forgiveness. All was going smoothly when, suddenly, unplanned words slipped spontaneously from my mouth: "In any given moment, we are all doing the best we can." The room fell silent; gazes dropped inward to consider what had just been offered. A few gentle smiles slowly emerged, as well as several skeptical glances. I considered what I had just said: *In any given moment, we are all doing the best we can.* I grew confident in those words and stayed with them. I realized that it was essential to say "In any given moment . . ." because in the next moment one's best might be much better. Yet, in a given moment, with the unique causes and conditions of that moment, we make the best decision we can. Later, I would write that phrase in my first book, and I have since received many grateful emails focused on that one statement—and, yes, a few questioning it.

For me, it was the beginning of accepting that even when I had behaved so poorly with Beau, my actions could be viewed through the lens of the causes and conditions of my life at that time. It was a bitter pill to swallow—that such unskillfulness was the best that I could do. Was I rationalizing unskillful actions or was I making an effort to practice self-compassion? I considered how Beau had never turned against me, and I decided to work on forgiving myself.

When Beau died, the sadness I felt was deepened by a sense of incompleteness. He and I still had work to do and now I would have to do it without him. People asked if we would get another dog. We didn't want another dog, we wanted Beau back. It was the classic scenario for creating *dukkha*—the suffering that comes from wanting something to be different from the way it is.

As time passed, the empty space in our home and in our hearts grew larger, and there was only one way to fill it. Dodger (the Artful one) entered our lives and systematically brought us to our knees. He was a handful—irresistibly beyond redemption. Beau, however, had taught me well, and I never lost patience during Dodger's long training period. It was my calm, forbearing, and loving care of Dodger that allowed me to ultimately forgive myself for my unskillfulness with Beau.

For many years I had thought I would never gain the freedom of self-forgiveness, but our furry companions can be persistent teachers. It is said that when you study with a master, there may be little time when they are actually speaking to you. The rest of the time, observe carefully how they peel their orange and how they put on their sandals. Therein lies the real teaching.

Beau never ate oranges, but occasionally he wore something akin to sandals. Here in New York, when it snows, building superintendents often sprinkle salt on the sidewalks to melt the snow. That salt irritates the delicate paws of dogs, so as Beau got older, we began putting little rubber boots on him to protect his feet. It was not his favorite thing, but once the boots were on I got several licks of gratitude. Even doing what the golden master didn't particularly like, he never wavered from his loving nature.

I can still feel the silky-smooth warmth of Beau's face in the memory of my hands. His teachings on love, compassion, joy, and equanimity remain with me, and I am so grateful.

ABOVE Zoe Mae

LEFT Milo and Ketzel

Against and Into the World

Ketzel Levine

I've never much liked staying in one place too long. Leaving is second nature when you never feel you belong. Knowing her as I do, Zoe Mae would agree. To this day, at age sixteen, my scheming, restless animal, with her Chewbacca-like looks and fierce agenda, still walks the fence-line of our sprawling dog park hoping to bust through a loosely latched gate.

Zoe Mae is an alleged F1-hybrid labradoodle with terrier-like intransigence and preternatural cunning. She was three years old when she came into my life. We were a reckless twosome from the get-go, two aggressively independent outsiders with no fixed sense of community and an unwise penchant for challenging terrain. So, when the inner call came to pack up and move to Ecuador, Zoe Mae was game.

Here was the long view at the time of our departure: my mother was six months dead, and I was in mourning, not simply for her, but for my career as well. My thirty years in broadcasting had come to an abrupt, subprime-mortgaged bust, and though I tried valiantly to reinvent myself—as a blogger, a horticultural tour leader, an Internet radio consultant, a multimedia storyteller—I succeeded only in becoming vegan.

The move to Ecuador was another attempt at reinvention. I had a dream, and it had a name: *Colegio de Perros*. I'd hoped to create an elite dog-training school using the best and brightest stray dogs in the region and working with big-name trainers from all over the world (who'd gladly volunteer their time to be spoiled with farm-to-table fare while living in a magnificent hacienda overlooking the Andes). The dog-college graduates would be sold for a mint—to good people, of course—thus helping fund the operation, which would be run by an army of volunteer vacationers (the waiting list would be epic!) plus, of course, my own full-time staff. In this way, I'd achieve a lifetime's yearnings in one fell swoop: save animals, create community, live a bilingual life abroad, and have a full-time cook.

My six months in Ecuador—groundwork for my *colegio*—did not go as planned. (Can you spell h-u-b-r-i-s?) My stay was crippled by my fantastical expectations of the expats I'd meet (Liberal! Open hearted! Charity minded! Animal lovers!) and the good works I'd accomplish (Spay! Neuter! Foster! Adopt! Humane education!). Two months into the experience of living in unsustainable isolation in an hacienda on the top of a mountain, accessible only by a wing and a prayer and a four-wheel-drive vehicle, I hadn't allowed for the truth of building community. (Rule #1: Live among people.)

That was one whole lack of vision. The other was the result of a retinal detachment while living at 12,000 feet. (The altitude was not the cause.) The surgery went without a hitch, but the recovery? Not so well. I had to wait a week before I could return to my high-elevation home, but with two dogs in my care and few friends, I had scant choices for a place to live. A canine-loving couple took in Filipo—a dog I'd adopted in Ecuador. Would that they'd taken Zoe Mae and me. We stayed with a Canadian couple whose initial kindness wore off inexplicably fast as I lay in their guest bedroom prone and immobilized per doctor's orders.

Talk about vulnerable! I was thousands of miles from anyone who loved me. Zoe Mae was more a source of worry than support. Taking her for a walk was treacherous given my kaleidoscopic vision and light blindness. We both needed a mommy. My big sister was actually *in* Ecuador while all this was going on, but she was traveling with a friend to prettier places. Why didn't she drop everything to come take care of me? Perhaps because I told her *not* to come? What was *that* about? When I was finally well enough to grab a dog-friendly taxi back up the mountain, I wrapped myself in my splendid isolation and sank into a spiritual abyss.

About a week later, my sister did show up. She sat by me as I fell apart; then she took me for a walk to town. We were a motley crew scurrying down a hairpin-turn road: two pied-piping *gringitas* and three *perros*, Zoe Mae, Filipo, and Brownie—a magnificent albeit undernourished yellow Lab from a neighboring farm.

We were on our way to a hole-in-the-wall cantina and ice-cold Cokes when I heard a god-awful scream and went running. A puppy was sitting stunned in the road—another hit-and-run dog day in Ecuador. A few locals looked on but no one was moved to help. The little guy was in shock and had shat himself, as I discovered when I scooped him up. My sister took the big dogs back up the mountain, while I snagged a forty-five-minute ride to the nearest vet.

Milo showed a whole different way of being.

Two days later, I brought the puppy home. The circumstances of our meeting seemed a miracle, so I named him Milagro. Loving him would save me.

I have long been a person like Zoe Mae, intense and unpredictable. But Milagro—or Milo, as he's now known—is an open book. People want to know the *kind* of dog Zoe Mae is, but people just want to *know* Milo. Zoe Mae is a force of nature; Milo is honeyed light. She stays on the edge; he wants to be in the center. She plots and plans; he lives amazed.

Five years after finding Milo, I have traveled an incredible journey with these two animals. Zoe Mae has not changed. She loves me—I know she loves me—but on our daily rural walks outside Portland, Oregon, if I want to hold onto her, she has to be leashed. Milo, on the other hand, runs off-leash yet is constantly turning back, checking in, staying near.

I miss living on top of a mountain, and I still have wanderlust. I may always struggle, to some degree, with learning how to belong. But Milo has shown me a new way, and I covet his delight being *in and of* the world. Zoe Mae is a survivor, a scrapper, and together we were sheltered, two against the world; Milo, *mi Milagro,* is my open door.

ABOVE Tilla and Stuart

Tilla, the Lake, the Sky

Stuart Davis

've had several dogs in my life. I've loved them all, but I do feel differently about Tilla, the Doberman pinscher our family cohabitates with. Tilla has a contemplative side to him, and his unique presence kindles the living dharma—the mystery of existence—for me.

I'll try not to get too anthropomorphic about it. It's common and tempting to project human ideals on canine behaviors, but some things about Tilla's way of being make it plainly evident he has a rich inner world, a great emotional sensitivity, and an attuned regard for the world around him. His nature to notice reminds me of mine.

From the time he was a young pup, Tilla has often stopped whatever he's doing to study a bird in flight. He considers the details in his surroundings with a pensive regard. His eyes take on the same wistfulness I feel when I'm transported by the sight of a crow or a mountain sunset. His curiosity is attuned to those moments, and when I'm with him I remember I'm exploring this mysterious, enchanted world.

When I was a kid I dreamed of other worlds—exotic exoplanets as they're called now. I imagined a time in humanity's future when interstellar travel might be possible, the discovery of intelligent beings, and the unimaginable surprise of what other life forms might be like. What would it feel like to share experience with a truly "other" sentient intelligence?

Now I realize I am, of course, actually living out that dream on this planet. I'm on exactly the kind of planet I always hoped to find. I walk the surface of a world that is part Garden of Eden, part apocalyptic Hell. My companion is a four-legged beauty of a beast whose thoughtful gaze communicates wordless meaning to me every day. I often ruminate about the way Tilla's and my life intersect, and what we're learning here. The dharma is every bit as much his native endowment as it is mine. Who's to say the dharma must come exclusively through anthropomorphic filters?

When I am able, for a moment, to fully appreciate that my consciousness found its way into my body, that I roam a planet teeming with life, and that I share my inner and outer reality with a four-legged canid, it's impossible not to be astounded. The precious human vehicle, the source and end of suffering, the condition of all beings—all of these riddles are informed by my friendship with Tilla.

He, too, is a conscious being who navigates suffering and an end to suffering. He too studies his interactions and the world around him, and through awareness and feeling he attempts to understand and learn. The love, pain, and other experiences he goes through shape his progressive development. That is a path of spiritual development. And all of that is how we mutually encounter living dharma.

I received Jukai (the Buddhist initiation ritual) from a Zen master who emphatically believed his dog to be a deeply awakened being that consciously incarnated to reduce the Zen master's suffering. He said the dog's death was the single hardest emotional event of his life—harder than when his family members or friends had died.

At the time I thought this was just an emotional story he was telling himself. Dogs are dogs, and people are people, and when we assign anthropomorphic qualities to pets, it speaks to our confusion, not to the pet's actual nature.

Now I feel differently. I don't think Tilla incarnated consciously to reduce my suffering. I do know he's a sentient being, and his experiences are shaping his change, and that my life and his are sharing in the living dharma in unique but consonant ways. That's profound. My views on whether or not my Zen master's dog was an awakened bodhisattva have softened. Who knows? Not me. I definitely get the way our dogs are not ornaments or even merely companions. The very same Ground of Being that animates precious humanity abides in Tilla.

Tilla moves through his life in a way that puts me in contact with the sense of wonder I've felt since I was first able to consider the vastness of the universe or the minuteness of its constituents. When I see Tilla fall into a deep gaze, absorbed by some feature of the moment I had missed, I often follow him in, back to where I actually am. *Do I do that for him?* I don't know. I do know we both feel love, affection, humor, curiosity, happiness, sadness, and a contemplative regard for life.

Sometimes if you sit with a dog at the edge of a lake and watch a bird, a bewildering miracle comes into focus. Wind, water, sky unveil the living dharma.

In the midst of it all, Tilla is at home, and I'm home with him. We are something, expressed from nothing, and the nothing that issues something—the dyad of void and form, the native endowment of every sentient creature.

> Life *is* meaning, and to live meaningfully is all that needs to be done. His nature to notice reminds me of mine.

There are more planets in the cosmos than grains of sand on Earth, and this one has intelligent life. It's teeming with trillions of creatures, sentient quadrupeds, self-reflexive bipeds, and highly intelligent cephalopod mollusks of the order *Octopoda*. I roam at will, explore on impulse, and am largely allowed to pursue and create whatever I like.

For most of human history, simple survival was the only game. Even now, through much of the world, it remains the central challenge. I, or Tilla, could have been born in a war zone or into conditions of dire suffering and oppression. It's baffling beyond measure, the opportunity I have. I'm healthy, safe, loved. I have these luxuries, and I wish them for every being alive.

The intelligent tenderness in Tilla's eyes reminds me not only to wish for that, but to take action to make it so.

Sometimes at the lake, when my wife and I watch Tilla run free—happy as he could possibly be—the meaning of it all is so clear. There is no meaning of life to be revealed. Life *is* meaning, and to live meaningfully is all that needs to be done. It's not even required; we're just invited. Tilla is fully alive, so completely present; he lives profoundly and helps me to do the same.

There are realms of inner landscape that only open up between beings, between species. It's through my connection with Tilla, a member of another species, that I can begin to feel how radically mind-blowing it is to be human and receive the gifts of Buddha, dharma, sangha.

Tilla is an important companion for where I still need to go on the inner odyssey. To continue waking, to seek the end of suffering for all beings. Every species, each creature. All the planets. They are numberless, but I vow.

That's where the magnet pulls, and if it weren't for Tilla, I might be more tempted to remain in the comforting familiarity of stasis. He's a loving disruptor, and loving him as I do, I care about his experience. And that makes me curious about other creatures on this planet we're exploring. His presence shifts my own.

Take vegetarianism for example. For seven years I was a vegetarian. My reasons were less about health and more about the emotional lives of animals. However, I married an omnivore, and over time I went back to meat. For a decade I was not a vegetarian, yet lately I'm feeling a need to return to it, and in large part it's been my relationship with Tilla that has nudged me. Knowing that he has such a rich inner world and is so full of feeling and contemplation, I'm reminded how every animal has their own emotional and inner life. Having them as my food creates a growing dissonance in my heart and head.

When I first started practicing Buddhism, I was really into reading books. They were great. I loved meditating many hours a day. It helped. Over the past couple decades, what has grown and deepened my life is the practice of family—of being a husband, a father, and a companion to Tilla. I'm under no delusion that I've arrived or become enlightened. Nope. But I do think family and my friendship with Tilla help me become more human.

These days I'm interested in sitting at the edge of the lake with my wife and Tilla as we watch a bird. I like feeling the inventive way living dharma twinkles in a Doberman pinscher's dark-brown eyes.

ABOVE Hopi (left), Beryl, and Nellie

My Hopi

Beryl Bender Birch

Ever since I was a child, when I had an imaginary wolf as my best friend, I wanted to have a real wolf. Understanding as I grew older that wolves are wild and aren't meant to be domesticated and kept as pets, I settled on a Siberian husky, the closest domestic dog to a wolf. Although she was 100 percent Siberian and her eyes were sky blue, my Hopi looked more like a small white wolf. A traditional "show" husky has a fluffy coat, curled-up tail, stocky build, and, of course, those masklike facial markings. Hopi had none of those traits. She was like a *field* variety of husky: fine coated, lean, and long legged with an extended, dropped-down tail. She was mostly white with a couple dark-gray spots.

Hopi came from a breeder in Massachusetts, a legendary musher and veterinarian who was renowned for his line of "racing" Siberians. He bred his dogs for speed, intelligence, and endurance, not for their markings, so most of them did not look much like the traditional husky. They all had good pedigrees and a long racing lineage that went all the way back to the Alaskan village dog—the predecessor of the Siberian husky—which descended eons before from *Canis lupus,* the gray wolf. I found the breeder after much research, and I hoped to buy a puppy from him, but he was fussy about who he sold dogs to. I wasn't a musher, and he didn't want to waste a potentially great sled dog by selling me one for a pet. I figured the only way I would ever get a puppy from this guy was to take a couple of his older dogs first and actually learn something about sled-dog racing.

First I bought two nine-year-old retired lead dogs—Anna and Snowflake—who became the founding members of my Retirement Ranch for Racing Siberians. Gradually I acquired all the

159

paraphernalia that goes along with running dogs: first a Toyota Tundra, then a six-passenger dog box to go on the truck bed, then an ATV for training, and finally a sled, harnesses, gang lines, drop lines, and everything else it takes to run sled dogs.

I spent a couple of winters training with a musher who had dogs from the same kennel, and with practice three or four days a week, I eventually became skilled enough to run four to six dogs a few miles without tangles, fights, forays off trail into the woods, or any kind of a general free-for-all. Finally, I was able to convince my breeder buddy that I had "earned" a puppy.

In the summer of 1997, my long-awaited opportunity to sit with a litter of twelve-week-old huskies arrived. I plopped down in the pile of puppies and waited for my soul mate to make herself known. Just then, one of the puppies came over with a stick in her mouth and dropped it in my lap. The wife of the breeder commented, "She's the only one who retrieves stuff. She is always picking up things and carrying them around. She isn't so interested in the other puppies. She is kind of a lone wolf!"

I picked up that little puppy and looked into her eyes. She looked right at me, and I swear in that moment we both remembered one another from many lifetimes together. It was the first of thousands of times I experienced what came to be known to me as "the long stare," a trait shared only by wolves and huskies.

Hopi and I spent twelve years together. When I began to seriously train and run dogs, primarily for fun and to exercise all the retired sled dogs I was accumulating, she ran as my lead dog. Much to my delight, she turned out to be one of the best dogs ever to emerge from the kennel where she was bred; she was born to run and loved it. She was a perfectly focused, perfectly configured sled dog and a natural leader. She slept with me every night, traveled with me, and went almost everywhere I went. She was my best friend, my mystical partner, and my teacher. She taught me again and again the essence of my spiritual practice: pay attention, be present, appreciate and be grateful for every moment of life, and celebrate impermanence.

Impermanence is a fairly difficult idea to wrap your mind around, mostly because we all tend to think that things will last. Humans don't like impermanence, unless of course we are in a situation that is uncomfortable. Then it's fine. But for the most part, we think that our things, our accomplishments—all the stuff we use to give ourselves a sense of individuality, a sense of who we are, like our jobs, parents, kids, pets, homes, and health—will be around forever.

We might *say* that we understand things don't last, but we don't really *get it*. According to many of the Eastern wisdom traditions, this is why we suffer. The Yoga Sutra, for example, says that *avidya*, or "ignorance," is the cause of suffering and is defined as the problematic inclination we humans have to confuse that which is impermanent with permanence. Because we expect things to last or not to change, we are stunned when they *don't* last or *do* change. We identify with and hang on to stuff in order to give ourselves a sense of who we are. We identify with what we have—*my* house, *my* car, *my* things—or what we do—I'm a runner, a stockbroker, a Democrat, a mother—and on we go. That becomes *who* we are.

All of those things will change. If our whole sense of self is tied up with being a runner or a mother, for example, what happens when we aren't those things anymore? When identities we have set up for ourselves change, and when the stuff we have accumulated disappears and we are forced to let go by circumstance,

> She taught me the essence of my spiritual practice: pay attention, be present, appreciate and be grateful for every moment of life, and celebrate impermanence.

what happens? We suffer because we are adrift without a clue as to who we are. So the whole point of practicing yoga, from a fairly sophisticated viewpoint, is to finally understand that nothing in the world of form is permanent, and if we want to be happy, we need to realize that the *here and now* is literally all there is. It is in that realization or that awareness of the True Self—which is the underlying, singular essence of all things and is *not* in the world of form and *is* permanent—that happiness dawns.

A powerful part of the yoga teacher training courses that my school directs is a ritual called Celebrate Impermanence that involves cultivating an understanding of this "letting go" business. In yoga, the practice of *vairagya*, or nonattachment, tells us that although it is fine to be passionate, involved, and committed, we also might want to rehearse letting go of our attachments little by little, as someday we will have to let go of everything. It makes dying easier! In class, everyone names something that they're attached to: family, job, home, health, morning coffee. Then we acknowledge that one day we will need to let go of everything each of us has named. I always named Hopi as the one thing I was most attached to. I have always known, of course, that one day she would die; I also always knew that letting go of her would be one of my most difficult assignments as a practicing yogi.

Hopi died of cancer just before Thanksgiving in 2008. We found the cancer about a year earlier. After a major surgery in March, when a primary tumor was removed and she was given a clean bill of health, two small metastatic tumors unexpectedly showed up on an X-ray in June. On the day that I found out about the return of the cancer, I decided I would walk with her every morning until the day she died. We would go out at around six o'clock to the beach or the bay. We walked just to walk. Not to get anywhere, not as a means to an end, or for any purpose other than to be outside with the sun and the wind and the seagulls and terns—and to be together. The mornings were filled with brilliant sunshine or dark clouds. The waters were sometimes still and clear, sometimes turbulent and vague. We sniffed horseshoe crabs and seaweed. We peed on driftwood. Every moment was sacred, timeless. We sat together and watched the piping plovers fish for breakfast. We smiled and said hello to the pebbles, the blue sky, and the geese flying overhead. We stopped and breathed. We both knew that one day the point of letting go, which I had talked about for so long in my workshops, would soon come. Rather than sadness, that knowing brought us to the present moment (well, not really "us," but me; Hopi always knew how to be present) and to an exquisite joy and fullness of life.

I was in Florida in the middle of a weeklong teacher training when I got the call from my dogsitter that Hopi wasn't doing so well. I changed my flight and flew home immediately, arriving just after midnight. I sat up with her the entire night. I lit candles and built a fire in the fireplace. She stood outside on the deck, gazing into the distance and breathing with a difficult, shallow-but-heavy rasping sound. With much persuasion, she would come in and lie down next to me on her bed, and I would hold her head in my hand, stroking her ears and eyes gently. She would fall asleep—she was so tired, yet she fought for life—and her breath would become silent and shallow. She would sleep, her head in my hand for twenty or thirty minutes, then wake up, her eyes big and a little frightened. I prayed her heart would just stop and she wouldn't wake up. But she was an athlete with a heart as strong as can be; it didn't happen. She would wake again. Then go stand outside—a freezing cold night—and just try to breathe.

At eight o'clock the next morning, I called the vet and we planned for him to come to the house around 11:30. Then Hopi and I went for a walk—out to her training grounds—acres and acres of fields where we trained for our races every winter. She trotted around a bit, stopping and standing in the middle of the fields with her head in the air, sniffing the wind, remembering all her runs. She came within fifty yards of a beautiful doe. They stood and regarded one another. In earlier days, Hopi would have been off like a rocket! We didn't stay long—about thirty minutes. She was ready to rest again. I told her it would be our last time together in these fields and that now she would go home, fall asleep, and go on to her next adventures. I told her to choose her parents carefully and not to be born as a starving or abused child or a suffering animal used for food or clothes or entertainment or medical studies to serve humans—to find joyful souls who would love her as I did, and as she did me.

The pain of her death was exquisite. I cried for weeks, but felt an indescribable joy and comfort that was an equal part of the grief. I was so grateful that I had spent time with her—*only* with her, fully present and joyful. I was grateful for my yoga practice in all its dimensions, and I was especially grateful to Hopi herself for helping me to bear the loss of my best friend and teacher, and to embrace her death and understand it as a natural, beautiful part of life—just as she had taught me. I was able, thankfully, to celebrate impermanence as I cried.

ABOVE Izzy, Geneen, and Matt

The Dog, and the Door Swinging Open

Geneen Roth

There are some mornings when I wake up with a mind that sounds like a shock jock. (Confession: I've never actually heard a shock jock, and I have no desire to because I'm pretty sure what he would sound like: my mind.)

For example: we just brought home a new puppy, whose red fur is soft and a bit curly. My friend Catherine says she looks like a person impersonating Lucille Ball. Although we wanted a dog who was *slightly* rambunctious, who pranced around and was very affectionate, we, by chance, met a cowering, abused, abandoned puppy who needed a home and decided we couldn't leave her.

So instead of a sassy, happy dog, we brought home a dog who was afraid of everything: doorways, dogs, people, water, toys, food, us. And the worst thing about all this was not the puppy, but my *thoughts* about the puppy. Every morning, my shock-jock mind would rant things like: "You've got the wrong dog. You are not nice enough to rescue a dog. You wanted a dog who prances, not a dog who cowers. It will take years to rehabilitate her, and you have more important things to do than that. Return her."

I was aware that I was suffering because I was wedded to my thoughts. I knew that should I choose to divert my attention from the tangle of thought to the field of the inner body, the nightmare would dissolve. Poof. Gone. Maybe then I would find something cuddly and loveable on the other side of the cowering, fearful little being we had taken in. But I didn't want to. For so long, I believed that the adrenaline and suffering were synonymous with aliveness itself. Freeing myself from the rant, still, at moments, feels like taking a leap into the unknown, like volunteering to dissolve. And therein lies the pickle (to the extent that one can call consciousness a pickle): How do you choose freedom from thought when thought is so compelling? How, when you are aware that you have a choice, do you choose freedom and therefore connection?

This much I know: During the times in my life when living in my mind was so obviously like living in a hell realm—when my husband and I lost our money, when I almost died from a medical procedure gone awry—and my thoughts were about shame and blame, choosing to stay present felt like a choiceless choice. If I wanted to get through the night (or day) without torturing myself, if I wanted to drink a cup of tea or walk outside in my garden with any degree of ease, riding the roller coaster of my mind was not an option.

And so, I kept placing my attention on sound, sensation, smell, sight. On taking one conscious breath, and then another. My dog, if I allowed, called me in to the present moment—the softness of her fur, the sweet vulnerability in her eyes, the sound of her tapping nails as she pranced across the wood floors. And every single time I'd land here, in the moment, it was as if I'd been given a ticket to a dazzling, bright universe of indescribable peace.

Although that profound ease of being has become more natural, sometimes, when I am not in a catastrophic situation (and let's face it, getting a puppy is not exactly catastrophic), the pull to believe my thoughts (e.g., I did it wrong; I am the wrong person; there isn't enough) is still magnetic. And what I know to do each time is to bring myself back to this exact moment. Whether it's losing my money or getting a puppy, the practice doesn't change.

So, a few days after we brought home our puppy, I realized I felt the way I always feel when I am wedded to my thoughts: trapped in a small, dark, airless room. And the puppy, in her sweetness, helped me realize I had a choice to open the door. In that moment of recognition, it was as if the door swung open and I stepped out into a lush garden-world that was shining and pulsing with life.

The sight of the goldfinch outside my window was breathtakingly gorgeous, even though I'd seen him bathing that morning and had walked by without stopping. My pen with the purple tip seemed luminous; the walls themselves were glowing. And then there was Izzy, our puppy. I noticed her, for perhaps the first time. I saw that once she mustered the courage to walk through the door to the backyard, she ran with a kind of wild joy. When she turned and pranced toward us, she kissed us as if we were who she had been waiting for.

The puppy, in her sweetness, helped me realize I had a choice to open the door.

Over the next few weeks, I saw that she, too, is emerging from cramped conditioning. And that there is always a moment, before she steps through a door, when she sits, looks around, and seems to consider whether or not to step into the unknown. But when she chooses to do it, the freedom and joy on the other side are wild and irresistible. Ten thousand kisses later, I've surrendered to The Izness (as we call her) and can say with some authority that the combination of kisses and consciousness is a winner.

A Dog Named
after a Boxer

Diane Musho Hamilton

On a meditation retreat more than fifteen years ago, I told my Zen teacher that I sometimes felt lonely. I expected him to offer me some compassionate guidance about working with my heart, and he did: he said I should get a dog. It was an unexpected piece of advice, but better than telling me to get a boyfriend.

A few weeks later, when my ten-year-old nephew was visiting for the weekend, I asked him if he wanted to look for a dog with me. He was thrilled, and pleaded for a boxer.

"C'mon," he said in his most persuasive tone. "Boxers are the best breed. Everybody loves them. They are buff, good-looking, and stand out in a crowd of other dogs. People think they are tough like pit bulls or Dobermans, but they are really nice. Really good with kids. I promise."

"I don't think so . . . "

I agreed that boxers were impressive, but I liked working dogs like border collies, blue heelers, or Australian shepherds. These dogs were bred to gather and herd sheep and cattle, and they are beautiful, ambling over the landscape for miles like coyotes with their limber shoulders and easygoing hips. They are great athletes, known for their quickness and agility. They may not be as handsome as boxers, but they're whip-smart and loyal in the extreme. They never run off because their every instinct is to keep the herd together—exactly my kind of dog.

So I told my nephew that even though I wouldn't get a boxer, I would name my new dog *after* a boxer. My offer was an attempt to assuage his disappointment, but it didn't diminish his longing for his kind of dog.

Nonetheless, we commenced our search. The local PetSmart held an adopt-a-pet fair every Saturday. We walked in together, and the first dog I saw was an Australian shepherd and blue heeler mix quietly sitting by himself at the end of a nylon rope. There was a lot of barking, whining, and general agitation in the pet store that day, but this dog was like a Zen monk, composed and calmly sitting by himself, gazing straight ahead. I knew immediately he was the dog I'd been looking for. After briefly checking out the other dogs, my nephew and I gathered the shepherd up and took him home.

Even though my dog seemed more like the humble Zen master, Ryokan, as promised, I named him "Ali," after the great heavyweight boxer, Muhammad Ali. The name didn't fit particularly well because my dog was as unassuming as Muhammad Ali was brash. While the great boxer was loud, audacious, and confident in the extreme, my new friend was quiet, unassuming, and self-contained. Muhammad Ali had a genius for building up the energy of a fight, while my Zen dog avoided confrontations with a deftness and subtlety I learned to admire. He could see aggression in a dog coming a mile away and would swing wide, staying aloof and free of trouble, all without breaking his stride.

I've heard some rescue dogs have a sense that their life has been saved and they are forever grateful. My Ali was like that; he wanted nothing more than to please me, and I often felt it was out of his sense of gratitude for rescuing him that day in the PetSmart. Muhammad Ali was not like that. A sports commentator suggested that he should be grateful—just as all black athletes of the time were supposed to be grateful to the white sports establishment for allowing them to compete at all. They were expected to be polite with the press and humble in the eyes of the public. Muhammad Ali changed all that. He expected his audience to be grateful to *him*—for his talent, beauty, speed; he knew he was the best thing that ever happened to the sport of boxing.

Muhammad Ali was far more than a great fighter. He was a true bodhisattva, someone with a profoundly awakened heart who manifested love and a great humor, and who sustained care for others. He continues to be a role model for young men around the world, some who live in poverty or worse, who need to see someone with his prestige to take a stand for their dignity and value. He gave them confidence that they could accomplish more in their lives no matter their situation. Many of his actions were in the service of a more just and fair world, including changing his name from Cassius Clay—which he regarded as a slave name—to Muhammad Ali, the religious name of a free man. He refused to be drafted during the Vietnam War and was convicted of draft evasion. Even though he lost four prime years of boxing competition, he stood by his principles, and eventually his conviction was overturned by the US Supreme Court. I read that the name Muhammad Ali means "one worthy of praise." Ali was the perfect name for the great boxer, and it was also the perfect name for my Zen companion.

My simple monklike dog had a tremendous heart. He was supremely devoted, and he showed me what a beautiful trait devotion is. I learned a lot about Zen practice observing how my dog comported himself. When I got up early and went to the Zendo to meditate, he joined me. When the *sangha* practiced late into the night, he was there with us. My most cherished memory of Ali is from our retreat center in the canyonlands of southern Utah. At the conclusion of each meditation period, when everyone got up from their cushion to begin the walking meditation, Ali would find his place in line with the rest of the silent practitioners and walk with us—easy, egoless, completely present. He modeled what the word "empty" means. He showed me how to be one with my experience. When he walked, he just walked. When he ate, he just ate. When he was sick, he was sick, drooling and bleary-eyed, until he was well again. And when he slept, he slept until it was time to get up again, and then he bounded to his feet without a moment's hesitation. I always admired that about him.

> When he walked, he just walked. When he ate, he just ate.

Ali was an extraordinary companion, and he loved me the way dogs do—clichéd, but true—without conditions. Because of his flawless friendship, we became inseparable. We took endless walks together, went on road trips, camped out, and hiked in the hills. He led me home once after I became lost in a snowstorm, rescuing me just as I had rescued him. I was grateful to Ali for that. I appreciated how much more time I spent in the wild mountains and canyons than I might have without him. Once, after a year or so together, someone asked, "What will you do when that dog dies?"

"I'll go back to being lonely."

Eventually, Ali did die. After fourteen remarkable years together, he grew old and faint, his hips gave in, and he passed. Like his namesake, he maintained tremendous dignity during his decline and continued to be generous in spite of his personal pain. A vet told me that my Ali had the most arthritic hips he had ever seen in a dog. He never complained, and no matter how long it took him to struggle up onto his feeble legs, he would—that is, until he couldn't. When he died, I was heartsick for weeks. My Zen training emphasizes the preciousness and the fleeting nature of our life, and I knew on the day I brought him home that one day he would die. Imagined loss is always different from the real thing, and grief is more real and demanding than I want it to be. I still miss my dog.

Muhammad Ali died at the age of seventy-four after many years of living with Parkinson's disease. He was a truly impressive human being, a sports icon, and one of the most beloved men of our time. My nephew has grown up; he is twenty-six now and has the handsome boxer he always wanted. He named the dog Bodhi, short for Bodhisattva. Recently, I got a new pup, too—another Australian shepherd who is just six months old. He is burly and brash, barking at anything that moves. He is nothing like Ali. This one is a fighter. Maybe I'll name him after the quiet monk, Ryokan.

ABOVE Rev. angel Kyodo williams

LEFT Legend

Dropping into What Is

Reverend angel Kyodo williams

had two dogs for a while—a pair of rottweilers named Lexus and Legend. They were very different personalities. What I learned from both of them was a very deep sense of *being with what is.* We all pine for things sometimes. Even dogs do, but they don't let their pining overtake them. They don't stay stuck in it and instead "relax into the situation," as Trungpa Rinpoche would say, which really was my takeaway, the wisdom from my dogs.

I used to live in upstate New York, not too far from Ithaca. It was very cold and snowed-in there every winter, even before climate change got to it. I was in a place in my life where everything had fallen apart. I was literally chopping wood and carrying water to keep myself warm and fed. I would take a chain saw and go cut firewood. My boy dog, Legend, never liked loud noises, and he was very protective. The first time I turned on the chain saw he looked like he was either going to lunge at it or take off. I stood there for a second because I couldn't quite figure out what he was going to do. Then I turned the chain saw off, petted Legend, and said, "It's okay." Then I picked up the chain saw and turned it on again. Legend tilted his head to the side, watching me, as if to say, "You're doing something with that." Then he sat down and looked at me the way he usually did whenever he was protecting our territory. He had found a place between his intense fear and powerful protection instinct and dropped into it—that place of "It's okay." It was quite amazing.

Lexus was very, very needy, and even her neediness was saying "This is just what I am, and take me how I am." She relaxed into it. She would come to me and want my attention really, really badly, and if she realized that she wasn't going to get it, she would relax. It was a dropping in. Dropping in, not separating it. Being with it.

In Buddhism, there's the animal realm that's supposedly beneath the human realm, but my sense is it's the other way around: dogs exist in some place between the human realm and the earthly realm. There's a relationship that they have that is deeply connected with the earth, where human beings are still struggling with the ongoing presence of nature and how it unfolds in front of us. I feel very strongly that dogs—and cats in their own way—are showing us that we don't have to wrestle with our world as much as we do—that we can be with it in a way that is really quite Divine.

We conflict and confuse *being with* what is with wanting to possess something. When I decided to be ordained as a Zen priest, I started on the path with a particular monastery that required people to leave their homes. I was determined to do this, but when confronted with the idea of leaving my partner and my dog (I only had Lexus at the time), I faced a dilemma. My partner could make her own decisions, but the dog didn't make the decision to be with me; I had brought her into my life and I couldn't abandon my commitment to her to chase this thing I wanted to do. I knew I could leave my partner, but I *couldn't* leave the dog.

So I didn't ordain in that tradition with that particular monastery because I had a commitment that was beyond me. I very much had a choice in that relationship, but Lexus didn't have the same options.

Legend and Lexus taught me that we are alive not to be owned and possessed by anyone, but to live fully. I was the one who adopted the dogs, and I was responsible. I can care for dogs and have the sense of commitment to them, and therefore, because of how that relationship is configured, leaving it would not have been an act of integrity. It wasn't because I owned the dogs—nobody can own a life force—it was something much larger. It's like having a great love, a great romantic love, and they pass out of your life and the loss of that great love is not "Oh, I should have had that and I should have gotten to keep it," but rather, "Oh, I never owned that to begin with." What I shared with my dogs was mine, but they are not mine.

In our society we understand love in some fairly limited forms: romantic love, filial love, and friendly love. Most of our love that goes beyond that seems to be more of an objectification of things, and I came to understand that a love that is rooted in a being's entitlement to receive love because it's alive was not one of possession. That is what I really experienced with my dogs. Even when I say "my dogs," I feel a little awkward, because they're "the dogs," and our relationship entitled them to have their own lives. When I lost them it didn't have as much to do with the loss of a possession as the loss of a *presence* in my life.

Their deaths were their wisdom gift to me. My dogs, even after they died, really helped me understand two things—that I could love, and that love is beyond human beings. In other words, it's that very deep sense of love that we carry and that lives within us.

Lexus died first, and then I noticed the deterioration in Legend, who I would say died of a broken heart. He was with his grief, and in many ways it seemed that his presence was a "what is-ness" because he really allowed himself to be in that.

> What I shared with my dogs was mine, but they are not mine.

Because I was unhooked from the idea that Lexus and Legend were possessions, when they died I knew I couldn't replace them. I loved them in a way I had attributed before to loving people. It wasn't "I had these things and I lost them," but rather "I lost something of myself." I'd lost a whole window through which to see myself, a way of relating, growing, and having a commitment to something other than myself. I knew that best when they were gone.

There was nothing I could say; there was nothing I could do that would make that sorrow go away. My love for the dogs was deeply unspoken, and all I had been able to do until that time was check to see how I was doing with this: *Yes, still in grief.* And be with it; I've been with it now for years. It has been a long time, and I can still feel my throat tightening when I think about it.

Ever since I lost Lexus and Legend I've been breathing space into that loss, but not really talking about it with many people. I had to *be with* the grief. Loss takes on a different quality—a more celebratory quality—when you appreciate that it is not the forfeiture of the possession, but rather the acknowledgment of the gift of what was.

ABOVE Sgt. Pepper (left), Ringo, Rachel, Laika, and Quila

Sgt. Pepper

Rachel Brathen

found Sgt. Pepper in a trash can, rummaging through garbage looking for something to eat. Only three weeks old, he was the sweetest, most gentle little being. Even though his belly was swollen from hunger and ticks, and wounds covered his body, and even though he was so weak he fell over when he tried to walk, he had life in his eyes. I took one look at his face and knew it was love. Unconditional love. Dennis would need some convincing, however. My boyfriend and I had only known each other for a few weeks, and getting a dog together is usually something a couple does after a few years.

I brought Pepper into our house, spent an hour cuddling and feeding him, then left him in a crate before I ran off to an appointment. Dennis would be home soon, so I taped a note to the crate: *Don't be mad—I'll explain later.*

Later, my boyfriend said that when he saw the crate he got so upset he didn't even look inside. "How could you go to the shelter and choose a dog without consulting me?" I explained that I hadn't been to the shelter; the sweet creature sleeping in the crate found *us*. All it took was one moment with Pepper, and Dennis knew it was true.

We went back and forth about his name for a while. What do you call an all-black dog with bright-blue eyes who refuses to sleep in his own bed, chews on anything he can find, chases imaginary lizards, and howls like a wolf at every high-pitched sound? Dennis wanted to name him Black Dynamite. I wanted to name him Yogi. We settled on Sgt. Pepper, from our favorite Beatles album

Sgt. Pepper's Lonely Hearts Club Band. As he got older his eyes went from bright blue to dark brown, and he grew into a big, muscular, Labrador-looking bundle of absolute joy.

Pepper became the center of our world, and it wasn't until we adopted him that we became a family. I already had Quila, a stray dog I'd picked up on a street in Costa Rica, and Dennis had Laika, a beautiful but somewhat feisty two-year-old pup he'd gotten from the shelter. Together, the five of us became a tribe. A few years later we added Ringo, a small pup. Six was the magic number!

For two years the six of us lived in our small house with a big garden on the island of Aruba, at peace with life. Dennis ran a skate shop and I taught yoga. Every afternoon we'd take all the dogs to the north shore for a long walk, and every weekend was spent on the beach playing catch, swimming, and chasing crabs. We had agreed that Ringo would be our last dog (four dogs in a small house is a lot!) but I still took in dogs from the street and cared for them, trying to find them homes. This was a risky thing to do as placing strays is never easy. Dennis had a two-week rule, which meant I had two weeks to find a home for any dog I rescued. If for some reason I wasn't able to, I'd have to take the poor thing to the shelter. The shelter is often full, due to the overpopulation of strays and unwanted litters on the island. Many of these animals end up in the government-funded "kill cage" and are euthanized. Luckily, we have found every stray a loving family thus far.

When Dennis and I got engaged, we knew we could never get married without having Pepper there. We got married in Sweden, where I'm from, and it was magical! Pepper and Ringo wore top hats and tuxedos. Dennis's best man and Pepper walked us down the aisle, but Pepper refused to sit down during the ceremony, confused as to why he wasn't right next to us. He barked and pulled on his leash as he tried to stand in between Dennis and me, so we shuffled some things around so that Pepper could be right there with us as we exchanged our rings.

After the wedding we spent a week at my dad's house paddleboarding on the lake, going for long runs, and enjoying time with the family. Pepper seemed a little low, and because he had been sick with a stomach flu the previous month and an ear infection just before that, we took him to the vet.

They couldn't find anything wrong with him, so we figured he was tired from all the excitement of the wedding and the long trip across the Atlantic.

We headed off on our honeymoon, leaving Pepper and Ringo with my dad to enjoy the Swedish summer, the lake, and the forest. While we were gone, Pepper again seemed a little down but was eating normally and going for walks with enthusiasm. My father took him to the vet, but again they found nothing wrong. Pepper visited four different veterinarians over the course of six weeks, but the diagnoses were always ear infection or stomach flu, and sometimes the recommendation was to feed him rice and lamb for a few days. My father said, "I guess he just misses you so much when you're gone," and I believed it.

After our honeymoon, Dennis, the dogs, and I flew back home to Aruba. For a few days, Pepper seemed to be his usual self, but then one morning we noticed something was wrong with his eye. It was bright blue—the same color it had been when he was a puppy—and he didn't seem to be able to see. The veterinarian in Aruba drew his blood and, knowing what to look for, told us he had a tick-borne disease. Pepper had probably been bitten before we left for Sweden. His blood count was so low the vet was surprised to see him standing up, let alone going for runs and eating big bowls of food. Four days later, Sgt. Pepper passed away. He was only four years old.

> I see him in the eyes of every dog we save.

Moving on after Pepper died was one of the most difficult things we've ever had to do. I felt extremely guilty for not having taken his initial symptoms more seriously and for not noticing how, even though he was active, he wasn't his usual self. The months that followed were awful. There was a big hole in our family and there were big holes in our hearts, and nothing could fill them. All I knew was I owed it to Pepper to do something good for the world to keep his legacy alive.

A dog named Omelet showed me the way. During a yoga retreat in Thailand, I came across a pit bull chained to a pole. Omelet's "owners" kept him restrained at all times, forcing him to live in a small concrete area in his own feces. I was heartbroken. Pepper's death was still fresh, and every dog

I saw reminded me of him. The day before I was supposed to leave the country, I knew I had to take action. I had no means of bringing Omelet out of Thailand, so I posted a photo of him on Instagram and reached out for help. I received more than five hundred emails *within a few hours!* People wrote from all over the world wanting to adopt him. Dennis and I did everything we could, but in the end we couldn't save him; the family that "owned" him refused to give him up.

Still, Omelet was a big catalyst for change. I started an Instagram account with the sole purpose of using social media for animal rescue. I named the account Sgt. Pepper's Friends, in honor of Pepper. How better to make him proud than to use this influence to save as many animals as I could?

The moment we returned home from Thailand, a stray puppy wandered into our garden. He was so dehydrated he could barely walk; cuts and scrapes covered his body. We took him in and named him Sammy. He turned out to be the very first rescue made by Sgt. Pepper's Friends. I posted his photo on the Instagram account and it worked! Hundreds of requests flooded in. Social media really is an amazing way to connect people and, apparently, animals as well.

Dennis and I knew that to make Sgt. Pepper's Friends a proper foundation and to create real change on Aruba, we were going to need some serious support. We partnered with two longtime animal-rescue workers, Melanie and Dayenne, and along with Amelie and Andrea, we established ourselves as a legal foundation. We were a team of six—the magic number! Sgt. Pepper's Friends now saves lives and rescues animals every single day. Animal rescue is so much easier when you have support from your community. Luckily for us, our community is filled with compassionate people from all over the world looking to open their hearts and homes to a new pet!

Losing Sgt. Pepper was one of the most difficult things I've ever had to go through, but I realize now that it wasn't for nothing. I miss him every moment of every day, but knowing that we are making a difference in the world in his name makes it all a little more bearable. Pepper inspired something profound and beautiful, and Dennis and I are so grateful for the time, however short, we had together with him. I think Pepper would be proud. Actually, I know he is. I see him in the eyes of every dog we save.

ABOVE Ziji and Fleet

Ziji's Dharma

Acharya Fleet Maull

My four-legged best buddy was Ziji, a purebred yellow Labrador retriever, and his dharma was clearly the transmission and gift of unconditional love. I loved him unabashedly and unconditionally from the moment I first saw him, and he returned my affection in no small measure. *Ziji* is a Tibetan word and Buddhist term generally translated as "unconditional confidence" or "brilliance" in the sense of shining or luminosity. From his puppy days, Ziji had a unique countenance or glow that attracted people's attention wherever he went.

He was definitely a "people" dog. He wasn't much interested in other dogs, and he found the alpha males a bit intimidating. Ziji was mostly interested in humans, and he always wanted to be wherever they were. He loved to go for walks and runs down the block, at the park, in the mountains, and especially on the beach—but he was not an outside dog on his own. He would never just hang out outdoors all by himself. He had to be wherever people were. Like most dogs, Ziji had a strong pack consciousness, but his pack was made up of humans, and he was never happy about one of those in his charge leaving the group.

Ziji did have two lifelong animal companions, a West Highland white terrier named Patti Smith and a dark-gray cat named Lou Reed. (Both were named by my housemate, Kate Crisp, a former punk-rock aficionado who is executive director of Prison Mindfulness Institute, a nonprofit organization I founded in 1989 while serving time.) Patti Smith loved to play and constantly tried to engage either Lou Reed or Ziji. As a puppy, Ziji cooperated a bit but soon lost interest; at best, he appeared to tolerate Patti from then on. This did nothing to deter Patti Smith's ardor for Ziji. She absolutely loved him, greeting him with great excitement and lavish attention anytime he'd been away, despite his indifference to her charms.

Ziji was loyal to a fault, especially to anyone possessing dog treats or food of any kind. His Labrador food addiction aside, he was definitely my buddy—a man's man—and would let me know any time I was being less than attentive. He was completely capable of pushing me off my computer when he wanted food, attention, or a walk, thus training me to be a less self-absorbed friend. He would also put his head on my thigh with the saddest puppy-dog look you ever saw, training me again and again to open my heart. Ziji was my lifelong teacher of both work–life balance and the value of getting outside to enjoy the elements.

When Ziji and his two companions were all ten years old, Kate and I moved our entire household from Colorado to Rhode Island, where Ziji became a sea dog. I'd sailed off and on during my life—at one time I captained a charter boat in the Virgin Islands—but Ziji, beach lover though he was, had never set paw on a boat. He fell in love with sailing the very first time we left the dock aboard *Innominate,* my gorgeous, black-hulled thirty-footer. Ziji would make himself at home, as happy as I'd ever seen him, and would spread out on one of the cockpit cushions, preferring, of course, the lee cushion when the boat heeled in a stiff wind. All I had to do was mention "going to the boat," and Ziji would jump around, his tail wagging vigorously. When driving or walking down to the marina, he could hardly contain himself in anticipation of getting out on the water. It was our shared meditation practice, especially during the long days of summer.

One day we noticed that Ziji had a growth on the back of his right front leg. The vet diagnosed it as a soft-celled cancerous tumor and warned that it could metastasize. We decided to have it removed, a successful operation. The vet suggested radiation treatments as a follow-up, but this felt potentially harmful and needlessly traumatizing for Ziji. Instead we did a lot of research and put Ziji on an anticancer-diet regimen of home-cooked meals—mostly natural turkey meat and vegetables. Ziji slimmed down considerably, which appeared to help his hip issues, common to Labs. The cancer never returned, and Ziji at times seemed as youthful as ever, running down the beach and dashing out into the waves to retrieve a stick.

As Ziji's physical decline became more apparent in his final years, my apprenticeship with him and his teaching entered an entirely new domain, challenging me to go ever deeper on the path of unconditional love, surrender, and grief. I am no stranger to this path. I lost my beloved teacher Trungpa Rinpoche two years into my fourteen-year sojourn in federal prison, my dad six months before being released, and my mom six months after. Just a year after being released from prison, I lost my former girlfriend and best friend, Karen, to cancer. Later, I lost Denise, my beloved partner of six years, to cancer as well. All this death, loss, and grieving seemed to inspire me to resist and deny Ziji's mortality and eventual passing instead of readying me for it. Nonetheless, in some inner way I was indeed preparing to let go of Ziji someday.

> He would put his head on my thigh with the saddest puppy-dog look you ever saw, training me again and again to open my heart.

I'd learned enough not to waste the moment or hold back my feelings. Ziji had always slept at the foot of my bed—on increasingly cushy dog beds over the years. Every evening before getting into my own bed, I would lie down next to Ziji, hold him, and tell him how much I loved him. If I awoke to find him gone, I wanted him to know beyond the shadow of a doubt how much I loved him.

My girlfriend, Sophie, moved in, and she and I and our housemate, Kate, began looking for a new place in the country to establish a training center for our prison mindfulness work. We envisioned a small farm with a barn we could convert into a meditation hall. As Ziji's physical condition worsened, we just hoped he would make it to the new home. Ziji struggled that winter, at times losing strength in his hindquarters and increasingly losing his hearing and sight. As the months passed, we became aware of Ziji's "last time" things: the last run on the beach, the last sail on the boat.

In April we moved from Providence, Rhode Island, to our new place in Deerfield, Massachusetts, on the north end of the Pioneer Valley. When the time came to pack up the household and caravan to western Massachusetts, we were all happy that Ziji was still with us and doing fairly well. Sophie, Kate, and I loaded up three cars and a U-Haul truck and hit the road with Ziji, Patti, and Lou Reed. That first night in our new home atop a hill surrounded by forest, we were struck by the profound quiet and peace. Under a night canopy ablaze with stars, we felt an immediate recognition of alignment. *This was it.* We were home, and Ziji had made it.

During the first two months of settling into our new place, Ziji got around okay but limped significantly on one leg. I got him a splint, and it seemed to help. He had the opportunity to explore several nearby parks along the Connecticut River. Kate was ever dedicated to giving Ziji the best quality of life possible. Then one day in June, while Kate was away on retreat, Ziji's hindquarters gave out altogether. He had no control over his back legs anymore. I got him a sling to help him stand to eat his food and go outside to do his business. Sophie and I did our best to make this work for a week or two, but then it became too hard for him to stand at all, much less go outside. I got some diapers and mattress protectors and set him up with a large, memory-foam bed in the living room. This is where Ziji spent his final days. We fed him by hand, but his normally insatiable appetite decreased daily. I continued to lie down next to him, to hold him, and to let him know how much I loved him and what an amazing friend he had always been. Who knows what our four-legged companions can actually understand cognitively, but it was clear to me that Ziji could "feel me."

As the days passed, Ziji's breathing became very shallow, and he was clearly afraid and suffering. I was still unclear about what to do. We were keeping his mouth moist with an eyedropper and taking turns being at his side so he would never be alone. Then Ziji had an episode of shaking and coughing up blood. Something in me said it was time to let him go and end his suffering.

I called the vet, who agreed to come over that evening. In anticipation of the doctor's arrival, we gently cleaned and groomed Ziji and arranged his bed in the living room to make him as comfortable as possible. Behind his bed, we set up a simple shrine on the sideboard under the picture window. When the doctor arrived, I didn't feel ready at all to let go of Ziji, but the momentum of the situation had set its course. After clearly explaining the steps he would take—first giving Ziji a sedative to relax him, then something to put him to sleep, and finally the injection that would end his life—the doctor asked if we were ready. Reluctantly, I nodded my head. Sophie, Kate, and I surrounded and held Ziji, gently stroking and petting him, expressing our love and gratitude, and saying our goodbyes. At some point his eyes closed and his breathing eased. He lapsed into sleep, and then he was gone. The doctor kindly and graciously excused himself and left us to sit with Ziji and our grief. I lay there with him for quite some time, immersed in a liminal world of intimacy, loss, love, sorrow, impermanence, and empty space. Ziji was gone after almost fifteen years of nonstop affection, love, and play mixed with lots of walks and naps and an insatiable appetite for treats of any kind.

At some point, my housemate brought meditation cushions and set up *puja* tables for practice. We all sat in meditation and performed various liturgies from the Tibetan and Shambhala Buddhist traditions, acknowledging the truth of impermanence and death, supporting Ziji's being in transition with lovingkindness and the blessings of our lineage, and honoring Ziji's life, his love for us, and our love for him through the ancient communal practice of sacred ritual and ceremony. I sat in meditation with Ziji late into the night, and we did another puja the next morning before preparing to transport Ziji's now-stiff body to a pet crematorium several hours away in Rhode Island. Patti Smith sat with his body too, honoring her brother Ziji, who never quite seemed to appreciate how much Patti adored him—although he did seem to soften toward her in his later years and final months.

On the two-hour drive to the pet crematorium, I shed a lot of tears, sobbed at times, and also laughed as I told Ziji stories. Upon seeing the crematorium's three, tall smokestacks spewing gray-white smoke, I had sudden flashes of Auschwitz-Birkenau, where I been leading retreats and bearing witness with the Zen Peacemakers for the past fifteen years. I was filled with dread to say the least.

The staff arranged Ziji on a rolling, cloth-draped, waist-high cart in a somewhat cheesy viewing parlor with faux statuary that really threw me over the edge. I was almost relieved when asked if I was ready, though in reality I was far from it. We wheeled Ziji into the back area where the ovens were and watched as they placed his body in the crematorium and closed the door. I left in a state of shock and irreconcilable grief and pain. Several hours later we retrieved Ziji's ashes sealed in a small wooden reliquary and then headed home to Deerfield. The ride was mostly somber and quiet, punctuated by periodic floods of tears and more Ziji stories.

During the weeks, and now months, since Ziji's passing, I find myself thinking of him, sometimes expecting to find him there at the door when I get home—playfully nuzzling my legs and wagging his tail—or waking in the morning with him at the foot of our bed. That small, wooden reliquary holding his ashes rests on the sideboard in the living room, close to where he passed from this life. A photo of him as a puppy is propped in front. The intention is to bury the reliquary here on the land with a small marker of some kind that honors my beloved friend and teacher, but I don't seem to be in a hurry to get it done.

Patti Smith and Lou Reed are still very much with us, and they bring delight in the unique ways in which our four-legged friends are particularly adept. Patti seemed disoriented for days after losing her lifelong companion. Sometimes I just sit and hold her in silent recognition; together we remember and honor our beloved friend, brother, and teacher. Ziji's absence, still painful, has left a very large hole in my life, and yet his legacy of unconditional love lingers, filling the cracks in my broken heart. Fortunately for me, it appears that Ziji, before he left, somehow convinced my partner, Sophie, to take on his job, nudging and guiding me along the path of love and surrender.

ABOVE Bunker and Julie

How Losing My Dog Helped Me Believe There's an Afterlife

Julie Barton

The most important relationship I've ever had was with my dog, Bunker Hill. He was a dark-red golden retriever, and I got him when we were both puppies: I was twenty-two and he was a mere few months old. I'd been recently diagnosed with major depression after a wicked and precipitous collapse, but the moment I held that puppy in my hands, my suicidal ideation stopped and sorrow seemed less immense. I knew it then, and I still believe it fervently: I had found my medicine and it came in the form of a dog.

For eleven years, I lived for Bunker. I thought about him every minute I was away from him and eventually got a job where I could bring him to the office with me. His presence, his essence, his joy, our connection: those things were my oxygen.

When, at age eleven, he got sick, I was pregnant with my second child. I was thirty-three and still utterly unsure that I could live without him. He died with his head in my lap, my eyes closed as I wept over him saying, "Thank you. Thank you." He'd saved my life. I felt his soul leave the room. When I opened my eyes, the light had changed. The blues were blander. The whites seemed gray. Bunker was gone, and I was pitched back into trying to live a life without my greatest source of comfort.

The day after Bunker died, I found out that I was a finalist in a prestigious writing contest. I hadn't been writing much and had entered on a whim. When I received that email, this thought popped into my mind: *Tell our story.* And, of course, I knew it was a message from Bunker. It seemed a wildly daunting task, but I thought maybe someday I'd write about us.

A few weeks later I took my enormous, pregnant self and two-year-old daughter to the park where Bunker used to lie in the grass and close his eyes and lift his head up in the air just a little, picking up scents and looking majestic, calm, at peace. Sometimes I tried to do the same thing just to channel him. Where was he now? How would I ever find him again? My daughter turned to me and said, "Can we go to Heaven's house now and pick up Bunker?"

Oh, how I wished I could've gone to Heaven's house and picked up Bunker. I missed him so fiercely. I felt as if I was half gone, like I was always forgetting something that was life-or-death important. Bunker's absence left a hole in my heart so big I feared I might not be able to manage a future without him.

I'm quite good at faking it through things. I can put on a nice smile. I know exactly what it takes to make someone think I'm doing just-fine-thank-you. Most chronically depressed people have this skill. I also had beautiful young kids who provided a welcome, if not exhausting, distraction. I can sustain this for quite a while, it turns out. But something huge was missing.

I'm not religious. I don't know if there's a heaven or not. It sounds nice, but the only thing I've ever really, truly believed in is nature. Trees and wild animals and dogs. They're my religion, my spirituality. So, was Bunker in the trees now? Was he in a bird? Was he in the moon and the sky? Where was my boy?

I didn't tell anyone, but I lit a candle and made an appointment with an animal psychic. I called her, clutching the phone with white knuckles. Could she find my boy? Could she tell him that I loved him and I missed him terribly? Could she tell him that I don't know how to really live without him? Could she tell him that I couldn't fake it much longer? Could she ask him how he's doing? And how I'll know if he's still with me?

She said Bunker's energy came in first. "Oh, here's a dog who really wants to come through. He has such great energy. He's so sweet. But he's crying. Oh no . . . He wants you to know 'I didn't want to go. But I couldn't stay.'" The lump in my throat was immediate. She continued using his words. "It was fabulous to be me. Can you imagine how good looking we were in our pictures?"

I laughed a little. Four months before he died, before I knew he was sick, I'd asked my photographer friend to take our photos at a local park. They had indeed turned out pretty nice.

The animal psychic continued, switching back and forth between his voice and hers. "He says, 'We locked and bonded. No one else could penetrate that.' It makes him cry, how grateful he is." She took a deep breath. "I feel his energy come and lay on my heart. It's amazing."

Her voice sounded dreamy and content, the way I felt when I was with him. I was supremely jealous. Why did she get to feel him after he was gone, yet I sat on the floor next to my lit candle with such deep emptiness that I couldn't be sure I'd make it through many more years of this life?

> I believe animals know more than we ever will about how the earth works, about how connected we all really are, about life, about death.

"Your two-year-old can still communicate with Bunker," she said. "Babies have the intuitive ability to speak to those who have passed."

I couldn't reply, just sniffle and wipe the big tears that had come. *Heaven's house.* Of course.

"I believe it," was all I could say. God, I missed him. The longing was crystalline in that moment: a tangible pulling inside my heart.

"Oh, and he wants you to know that he thinks his claim to fame was the huge party you had for him."

I thought for a while, but couldn't figure out what she meant. In fact, my heart sank a little because I'd put so much faith and hope in this pet psychic. We didn't actually have a party to celebrate Bunker's last day. My husband, Greg, and I bought him a steak and gave it to him on the patio, but there was no grand exit. It was sad and awful, and I still wasn't sure I'd done the right thing.

I thanked her for the call and berated myself for the strange lengths I'd gone to so that I wouldn't have to face this loss. I forgot to ask the psychic how to know if Bunker was still with me as I went about my days. I forgot to ask her to tell him that I needed signs. I needed something. "Anything," I said, aloud, while still sitting on my floor, looking at that candle, praying to the center of that light. "I need something, Bunker."

Then I remembered that we'd had a party for him when he was less than a year old—the Bunker Kegger, we called it. When I found out he had debilitating hip dysplasia and he needed expensive, life-saving surgery, my then housemates and I had hosted a keg party with a picture of Bunker next to a donation bucket. Bunker meant *that* party!

So I believed. I couldn't do anything else, could I? I spent a few more moments staring into that candle and decided that the writing contest news the day after he died had to mean something. *Tell our story.* I promised myself and Bunker's box of ashes that someday I would.

I believe animals know more than we ever will about how the earth works, about how connected we all really are, about life, about death. Whales follow the whale road, birds and butterflies turn the exact right way at the exact right time on the exact right day. Some Native American cultures believe that wolves howled the moon into being. Isn't that beautiful?

I looked at the moon those days, wondering if my boy was up there somewhere. And I wrote about the moon and the trees, about how I felt so connected to all of them. I found comfort walking quiet trails in the woods, listening to the birds, watching the moonrise.

So, in my grief, I did two things: I walked and I wrote. I wrote about every Bunker memory I could conjure. I lived for those short but meaningful writing sessions, recalling how, when he was alive, Bunker noticed my sorrow and leaned against me. I wrote about how consoling that was. I cried about how very lonely I felt without him. I usually wrote at my dining room table, which has a window that looks out at the inside of a huge New Zealand tea tree, a Leptospermum. I started noticing that when I wrote, little birds clung to my window frames, and other birds visited, especially huge, blue birds—Steller's jays and scrub jays. I went on hikes and found feathers lying in the center of my path. Blue feathers presented themselves even when I was walking in the middle of a dense city, so I decided that they were messages from Bunker. When a blue bird would land on the tree, I'd smile, say aloud, "Hi, Bunker. I miss you." I'd put one hand on my heart and offer gratitude. It was something, at least.

This morning, when I woke up with the intention to write this essay, I sipped my coffee and saw two Steller's jays and one scrub jay frolicking in the tea tree. "Hi, bud," I said. "I miss you." And just a few moments ago, a small brown sparrow clung to the window frame, flapping its wings. You don't have to believe me. I'm a skeptic, too. Always have been. But too many beautiful coincidences have happened for me to not trust that my boy is out there somewhere, watching over me.

I tend to have my best writing days around the full moon. I joked about it with my friends, saying I must have been part werewolf, or at least wolf. I decided to look at the phases of the moon when Bunker was born. I wrote a memoir about us, and the moon became one of the biggest metaphors. I soon discovered that the moon was always aligned with Bunker and me. I received the first box of my books ever on the blue moon. The publisher (with no assistance from me) scheduled the book to come out on July 19, 2016, a full moon. Then on August 17, the next full moon, I got a phone call from the publisher saying that the book about Bunker, the book I'd written to heal my grieving heart, had just become a *New York Times* bestseller.

Just now, I decided to look up the phase of the moon on the last night of Bunker's life: April 3, 2007. It was a night that I lay on the floor next to him, weeping, dreading, terrified of the prospect of living life without him. He licked my cheeks, swallowed my tears for me, even when he was terminally ill with too-far-gone cancer.

Yes, it turns out that the moon that night was full. So here I am writing again, shedding more tears at the miracle of it all, this deep connectedness. It has been almost ten years since I lost my Bunker and I'm still discovering magic about him, this biggest gift of my life, this beautiful being who saved me, who completed me, who has convinced me that there's something beautiful even in death. Maybe even a peaceful, quiet house belonging to Heaven who, I imagine, is very likely a sweet and loving golden retriever.

LEFT   Zuzu and Mark

TOP RIGHT   Saba and Mark

BOTTOM RIGHT   Mira and Mark

The Work of the World

Mark Nepo

The sun god decided to create new people. First he made a man,
then a woman, and finally a dog to keep them company.
from Folk Literature of the Tebuelche Indians

You think dogs won't be in heaven? I tell you, they will be there long before any of us.
Robert Louis Stevenson

When less than a year old, I was bitten by a Dalmatian. I have no memory of this. But as far back as I can remember, I had a strong, involuntary fear of dogs. It was my well-guarded secret all through school to avoid the cruel teasing of classmates. I developed a sixth sense. Always on guard, I could hear the jingle of dog tags a block away.

It was surviving cancer in my mid-thirties that loosened this fear. Landing back in life, completely transformed, tender and raw, I was strolling through Marigot in French St. Martin, a sleepy Caribbean town overflowing with lazy stray dogs. It occurred to me that I might no longer be afraid. So I walked by a small pack of street dogs, and for the first time in my life, I was bending down to pet a dog.

Three years later, for my fortieth birthday, my former wife, Ann, gifted me with a golden retriever pup. We picked her up at the breeder's farm, and she slept in my shirt the whole way home. I named her Saba, for the mystical resilient island I could see from St. Martin. Very quickly, Saba led this city boy into nature. Following her along trails and deep into woods, I discovered streams and clearings I would never have known without her.

But it was her first run in snow off-leash that changed me. She dashed with complete abandon and joy into an iced pond and I, without thought or hesitation, leapt in after her. My dear friend Paul was with me, and we stopped at a farmhouse and used a hairdryer on her for two hours to stop the chill. While riding home with Saba on my lap, I realized I had come to love what I feared.

Imagine the scraggly gray wolf that circled the first caveman who threw him scraps, and how they found affection for each other. Little did either know what they were beginning and how this lineage would strengthen the kindness and affection of both dogs and humans.

When we divorced, I agreed to leave Saba with Ann. She needed our dog more than I did, but it broke my heart. Years later, when in our first home, it was my wife, Susan, who wanted us to have a dog together. We held Mira, a yellow Lab, before her eyes opened. For thirteen-and-a-half years, she was our dog-child, our furry person, the innocent angel who nuzzled us when we were sad or hurt or sick. When Mira was about three, I wrote this poem:

The Deeper Chance

Mira is our dog-child.
And though we held her as a pup,
she has a need to be held
that comes from beyond us.
Though I sat with her when
she was the size of a loaf of bread,

sat on the kitchen floor staring softly
into her eyes, she has a need to stare
that comes from a place beneath
the awkwardness of humans.

These days, she seems a furry naked
thing that never looks away.

Now, I understand: God made the animals
as raw breathing elements, each closer
in their way to one aspect of being.

And that the friction of time on Earth
might have its chance to make us wise,
God made the animals speechless.

We've learned that Mira in Spanish
means to look. And lately, she licks us
awake and stares deep into us, as if to say,
Get up. Don't look away. Admit
you need to be held.

Four years ago, Mira died in our living room, in our arms. It was the most devastating loss Susan and
I have experienced. For a year and a half, we were lost in the dark pocket of that loss torn open by
her going. Her presence was everywhere; still is.

In time, we were caught between two awkward seasons: not sure we could ever have another dog in our home, and not sure we could go the rest of our lives without another dog. It was then that Susan saw a picture online of a yellow Lab rescue. About a year and a half old and marked with scars, she was found on the streets of Kentucky. We drove to a small town in Indiana south of Chicago to meet her. A week later, we brought her home. Susan named her Zuzu, after Zuzu's petals in the James Stewart classic movie *It's a Wonderful Life*. The name pointed to a second chance for all three of us.

Straightaway, we learned that Zuzu suffered trauma from living on the street. Within a month, I wrote this prose poem:

The Only Task

We weren't ready for another dog but there she was and we said yes. That first afternoon, her ball went under the couch. I used a yardstick to get it and she cowered. I held her softly, saying in her ear, "No one will ever hit you again." Within days, we discovered she's afraid of other dogs. Probably had to fight for food. Now she digs in at every sudden move. We weren't ready for this. But here we are, working to teach this loving creature not to dig in, not to be afraid. Struggling to assure her that she's safe. Humbled that I, who was afraid of dogs as a boy, am asked in my sixties to teach a dog not to fear other dogs. I'm stunned at how the choreography of fate is exquisitely disguised as chance. Zuzu is asleep beside me, her eyes twitching as she dreams of her instructions. Sent by the fates, like all the innocents, to find the ones who are afraid and help them teach others not to be afraid. It's the work of the world.

In the roots of my heart, I believe our dogs somehow know and sense each other. The first night we had Zuzu, she romped around the house, only to stop and stare at a portrait of Mira. After a long silence, she let out a slow yelp that wasn't a bark or a growl, but some otherworldly sign. The next day, I found Zuzu on her back happily playing with a toy, her tail wagging, when I realized she was in the exact spot on our living room floor where Mira died. It startled me into a mix of joy and sorrow. Then I collapsed into a long moment of awe. That seam between worlds of one life beginning in the exact spot where our beloved Mira left has been with me ever since, evoking a strange holiness that overwhelms me at unexpected times.

The choreography of fate is exquisitely disguised as chance.

In the Lenape tribe of Delaware, there is a legend that an orphaned boy found a starving pup and named him Witisa, which means "friend." The pup grew into a strong dog with mystical powers. When the boy fell ill, Witisa turned him into a dog, so they could run and hunt and survive together. Once the boy was well, Witisa restored him to his humanity, and said, "You have been kind to me and reared me. We will be pals for a lifetime."

This is what dogs do for us whenever we watch them run for the bliss of running. This is how dogs bring us into nature whenever we walk them and forget we are walking. This is how these magical guardians of the moment open the moment when we are trapped in our heads. Every morning Zuzu races around the yard until ecstatic, then sits before me, wanting me to run with her. It's her unfiltered love of the air, of the run, her wanting to stay close to me, that restores me no matter the weight I carry.

When I lost my dear friend Nur to cancer while just repairing from my own, it was Saba who taught me to feel that loss and let it sink into my heart. She did this on a walk in a cornfield when she played with a sheep's skull intensely, only to drop it and chase a butterfly. And when I broke Mira's paw by accidentally stepping on it when she was five—a break that needed surgery and which made her arthritic—it was Mira who taught me to accept my limitations, who taught me to forgive myself, though I still wince at having hurt her. She did this by licking my face every time I'd hang my head for having caused her pain. And when I'm stalled by my own recurring fears, it is Zuzu who teaches me that staying close to those I love calms me. She does this by needing me to stay close, by needing me to remind her ten times a day that she is safe and that I'm not going to leave her.

What more could I ask of these furry, mute sages than to teach me how to filter loss so I can keep living, how to accept my humanness so I can stay loving, and how to calm the fears that seem to never go away?

These three dogs have been my teachers: Saba, Mira, and now Zuzu. I am more loving and more in the world because of their dogness, their unstoppable presence, and their unending love. Like Witisa in the Lenape legend, each has turned me into a dog for a time, which has made me a better human.

Photo Credits

About the Contributors

Adyashanti is an American-born spiritual teacher devoted to serving the awakening of all beings. His teachings are an open invitation to stop, inquire, and recognize what is true and liberating at the core of all existence. His books include *Emptiness Dancing*, *The End of Your World*, *True Meditation*, *The Way of Liberation*, and *Falling into Grace*. Asked to teach in 1996 by his Zen teacher of fourteen years, Adyashanti offers teachings that are free of any tradition or ideology. "The Truth I point to is not confined within any religious point of view, belief system, or doctrine but is open to all and found within all." For more information, please visit adyashanti.org.

Julie Barton is the *New York Times* bestselling author of *Dog Medicine: How My Dog Saved Me from Myself*. She has an MFA in writing from Vermont College of Fine Arts and a master's degree in women's studies from Southern Connecticut State University. Nominated for a Pushcart Prize, Julie has been published in *Brain, Child*; *South Carolina Review*; *Louisiana Literature*; *Two Hawks Quarterly*; *Westview*; and *The Huffington Post*. She lives in northern California with her husband, Greg, two children, and small menagerie of pets. Read more about her at byjuliebarton.com.

A Harvard-trained scholar of comparative world religions, **Sera Beak** spent decades investigating spirituality around the globe, including studying with Sufi dervishes, Tibetan monks, Croatian mystics, shamans, and more. Sera is the author of *The Red Book: A Deliciously Unorthodox Approach to Igniting Your Divine Spark* and *Red Hot and Holy: A Heretic's Love Story*. Her shorter writings have appeared in *The New York Times*, *People*, *Publisher's Weekly*, and numerous other publications. She has made guest appearances on NPR, *The Dr. Oz Show*, and *Oprah and Friends*. Sera is noted for her playful and highly feminine approach to spirituality. She teaches at universities, churches, and retreat centers such as Omega, Kripalu, and Feathered Pipe Ranch, using a dynamic blend of creative exercises, meditation, journaling, and dialogue to help women find the sacred in themselves and their lives. Find out more at serabeak.com.

Sarah C. Beasley (Sera Kunzang Lhamo) is a Vajrayana Buddhist practitioner who spent more than six years in meditation retreat under Lama Tharchin Rinpoche and Thinley Norbu Rinpoche in the Santa Cruz Mountains. A teacher and writer, Sarah offers a workshop called Meditations for Death, Dying, and Living based on the Vajrasattva Ceremony for the Dead (Concise Nay Dren). Visit her website at moondropmeditation.com.

Beryl Bender Birch graduated from Syracuse University with a degree in English and philosophy. She has been an avid student of classical yoga since 1971, and she traveled to India in 1974 to further her studies. She is the founder/director of The Hard and the Soft Yoga Institute and cofounder and board chair of the Give Back Yoga Foundation. Beryl has been teaching yoga and training yoga teachers as "spiritual revolutionaries" for forty years and is the bestselling author of many books on yoga, including *Power Yoga* and *Yoga for Warriors*. Learn more at power-yoga.com and givebackyoga.org.

Rachel Brathen is the *New York Times* bestselling author of *Yoga Girl*, an inspirational cross-genre self-help/memoir/adventure story that traces her journey from troubled teen in Sweden to jungle explorer in Costa Rica to renowned yoga teacher on the Caribbean island of Aruba. Her yoga style focuses on a dynamic version of Vinyasa Flow that combines alignment, core work, and breathing techniques with basic poses. Rachel founded oneOeight.com, an online platform for yoga, meditation, and healing that became the most successful, crowd-funded yoga project of all time. More than two million people follow Rachel on social media, where she shares inspirational thoughts on yoga, health, meditation, and her own personal style of fearless living. Visit her website at rachelbrathen.com.

Lama Surya Das is one of the most learned and highly trained American-born lamas in the Tibetan Dzogchen tradition. For more than thirty years, he has studied with the great spiritual masters of Tibet, India, and Asia. Born Jeffrey Allen Miller, he left home for college in the 1960s, went to Woodstock, marched in antiwar rallies in Washington, graduated Phi Beta Kappa from SUNY–Buffalo, then went to India and Asia on a spiritual quest. Lama Surya Das is the founder of the Dzogchen Foundation and the author of many books, including *Make Me One with Everything*, *Awakening the Buddha Within*, and *Awakening to the Sacred*. Information about events with Lama Surya Das is at surya.org.

Musician **Stuart Davis**—called "one of the most fascinating and exceptional songwriters in modern music"—released his fifteenth album in 2012, followed by a tour of more than 130 cities in North America and Europe. His ground-breaking TV comedy series, *Sex, God, Rock 'n Roll*, can now be streamed on Amazon and led to a companion book by the same title. Davis often makes guest appearances on NPR's *Weekend Edition*, *World Café* with David Dye, *Coast to Coast* with George Noory, and other radio shows. A practicing Buddhist, Stuart is a charter member of Ken Wilber's spiritual think tank, Integral Institute (II), and contributes to its multimedia sister site, Integral Naked. Stuart is particularly fascinated with integrally informed linguistics. He lives on a houseboat in Amsterdam with his wife and two daughters. Find out more at stuartdavis.com.

Chris Grosso is a public speaker, writer, spiritual director of Toivo by Advocacy Unlimited and author of *Indie Spiritualist*, *Everything Mind*, *Dead Set On Living*, and *These Beautiful Wounds* (2018). He writes for *Origin* magazine, *The Huffington Post*, and *Mantra Yoga + Health*, and has spoken and performed at Wanderlust Festival, Celebrate Your Life, *Yoga Journal* conference, Sedona World Wisdom Days, Kripalu, Sun Valley Wellness Festival, and more. Chris is passionate about his work with people who are in the process of healing or who struggle with addictions of all kinds. He speaks and leads groups in detoxes, yoga studios, rehabs, youth centers, Twelve-Step meetings, hospitals, conferences, and festivals world-wide. He is a member of the advisory board for Drugs Over Dinner, and he hosts *The Indie Spiritualist* podcast on the Be Here Now Network. Visit his website at theindiespiritualist.com.

Roshi Joan Halifax, PhD, is a Buddhist teacher, anthropologist, and writer who has worked with dying people since 1970. She has been on the faculties of Columbia University, the University of Miami School of Medicine, The New School for Social Research, Naropa University, and the California Institute for Integral Studies. Her books include *The Human Encounter with Death* (with Stanislav Grof); *Shamanic Voices*; *Shaman: The Wounded Healer*; and *The Fruitful Darkness: Reconnecting with the Body of the Earth*. She founded both The Ojai Foundation (an educational center) and Upaya (a Buddhist study center in Santa Fe). In 1994, she created the Project on Being with Dying as a way to train health professionals in contemplative care of the dying. Learn more about the Upaya Zen Center at upaya.org.

Diane Musho Hamilton is a teacher of Zen and Integral Spirituality, an author, professional mediator, and facilitator. She has been a practitioner of meditation for more than thirty years and is a lineage holder in the Soto Zen tradition. Diane lives in Utah, where she is the executive director of Two Arrows Zen, a center for Zen study and practice, established in 2008 with her husband, Michael Mugaku Zimmerman. Diane is considered a pioneer in articulating and applying the insights of an Integral Life Practice based on the work of Ken Wilber. Since 2004, she has worked with Wilber and the Integral Institute in Denver, Colorado. In 2012 she cofounded Integral Facilitator, certifying practitioners in a developmental approach to group facilitation. She is the author of *Everything Is Workable: A Zen Approach to Conflict Resolution* and *The Zen of You and Me: A Guide to Getting Along with Just About Anyone*. She also contributed to *The Hidden Lamp: Stories from Twenty-Five Centuries of Awakened Women*. Her website is dianemushohamilton.com.

Andrew Holecek has completed the traditional, three-year Buddhist meditation retreat, and he offers seminars internationally on meditation, dream yoga, and the art of dying. He is the author of *Dream Yoga* (book and audio course); *The Power and the Pain: Transforming Spiritual Hardship into Joy*; *Preparing to Die: Practical Advice and Spiritual Wisdom from the Tibetan Buddhist Tradition*, and *Meditation in the iGeneration: How to Meditate in a World of Speed and Stress*. His work joins the knowledge of the West with the wisdom of the East to help us realize our full human potential. Andrew holds degrees in classical music and biology, and he earned a doctorate in dental surgery. He lives in Boulder, Colorado. See andrewholecek.com for more.

Pam Houston is the author of two novels, *Contents May Have Shifted* and *Sight Hound*, two collections of short stories, *Cowboys Are My Weakness* and *Waltzing the Cat*, and a collection of essays, *A Little More About Me*. Her stories have been selected for volumes of *The O. Henry Prize Stories*, *The Pushcart Prize* (2013), and *Best American Short Stories of the Century*. She teaches in the Low Rez MFA program at the Institute of American Indian Arts, is professor of English at UC–Davis, and directs the literary nonprofit Writing by Writers. She lives at 9,000 feet above sea level near the headwaters of the Rio Grande. The essay included here is an excerpt from her forthcoming memoir, *The Ranch: A Love Story*. Read more of Pam's work at pamhouston.wordpress.com.

American radio journalist **Ketzel Levine** became known as the "Doyenne of Dirt" for her ten-year stint as NPR's horticultural reporter on *Weekend Edition* with Scott Simon as well as senior correspondent on *Morning Edition*. Her writing has appeared in *Horticulture* magazine, *Martha Stewart Living*, and *The Oregonian*. A collection of her weekly columns was published in book form as *Plant This!* Ketzel was famously laid off from NPR while working on a documentary series about Americans coping with job loss and fallout from the 2007–08 financial crisis. Following her layoff, Levine began pursuing a lifelong interest in animal welfare and animal rescue. She currently teaches at the University of Oregon.

Allan Lokos is the founder and guiding teacher of Community Meditation Center in New York City. He is the author of *Patience: The Art of Peaceful Living*; *Pocket Peace: Effective Practices for Enlightened Living*; and *Through the Flames: Overcoming Disaster through Compassion, Patience, and Determination*. His writing has appeared in *The Huffington Post*, *Tricycle* magazine, Beliefnet.com, and several anthologies. Among the places Allan has taught are Columbia University's Teachers College, Albert Einstein College of Medicine, Omega Institute, Milken Institute, Barre Center for Buddhist Studies, Marymount College, The Rubin Museum's Brainwave series, BuddhaFest, New York Open Center, Tibet House, New York Insight Meditation Center, and Insight Meditation Community of Washington. Find out more at allanlokos.com.

Since beginning her arts career in the '70s in Los Angeles and '80s in New York City, **Susan Martin** has worked with prestigious galleries and museums, performance venues, and issue-oriented nonprofits to curate, produce, and promote books, performances, exhibitions, and special events with ground-breaking cultural creators like Laurie Anderson, Rhys Chatham, Lucinda Childs, Karen Finley, Philip Glass and his ensemble, Jenny Holzer, Meredith Monk, Nam June Paik, and Robert Wilson. Susan is the founding director of Some Serious Business, an innovative, artist-based organization known for presenting visionary artists and thought leaders. She's also creative consultant for Howl! Happening in New York City. Her diverse areas of expertise and experience do more than simply coexist—they are the foundation for a deep commitment to the transformative power of gratitude, generosity, an open heart, and the unified field of energy and creativity in all things. For information about Some Serious Business, visit someseriousbusiness.org.

Acharya Fleet Maull is an author, consultant, trainer, and executive coach who facilitates deep transformation for individuals and organizations through his philosophy and program, Radical Responsibility. He is a tireless, dedicated servant leader working for positive social transformation as a meditation teacher, consultant, trainer, social entrepreneur, peacemaker, and end-of-life care educator. He is an empowered senior teacher in two meditation traditions, a holder of the Way of Council, and a certified trainer with Partners in Leadership, New Line Consulting, Prison Mindfulness Institute, Center for Mindfulness in Corrections, and The Event training. Learn more at fleetmaull.com.

Mark Nepo continues to move and inspire readers and seekers around the world with his bestselling *The Book of Awakening*. He has published eighteen books and recorded thirteen audio projects; his work has been translated into more than twenty languages. His most recent books are *The Way Under the Way: The Place of True Meeting* and *The One Life We're Given: Finding the Wisdom That Waits in Your Heart*. He has created a video online course called *Flames That Light the Heart: Ten Lessons on Living with Meaning, Truth, and Kindness*. Read some of his poetry at marknepo.com.

Writer and painter **Jeri Parker** grew up scrambling along riverbanks and forest paths at her grand-parents' sawmill near West Yellowstone. Her days there were spent spinning logs on the millpond and fly-fishing on the Henry's Fork. If it rained, Jeri, her twin sister, and their cousins went to the cookhouse and made up stories about their future. Jeri never lost the habit of telling stories. They are now as likely to deal with the past as the future. Her memoir, *A Thousand Voices*, was published to critical acclaim and nominated for a Reading the West book award. Her novel, *Unmoored*, won the 15 Bytes Book Award for Fiction. Her other work includes *Uneasy Survivors: Five Women Writers* as well as short stories and poems in literary journals. Her paintings are in collections throughout Europe and the United States. She lives in Salt Lake City. Find out about her books and art at jeriparker.com.

Laura Pritchett is an American author whose work is rooted in the natural world. Her four novels have garnered numerous national literary awards, including PEN USA Award, the High Plains Book Award, the Milkweed National Fiction Prize, and the WILLA. She's published many essays and short stories in magazines, including *The New York Times*, *The Sun*, *High Country News*, *Orion*, and others. Laura's most recent novel is *The Blue Hour*, and she has a forthcoming nonfiction book titled *Making Friends with Death (Kind Of): A Guide to Your Impending Last Breath*. Her website is laurapritchett.com.

Joan Ranquet is an animal communicator and energy healer who teaches basic and advanced work-shops nationwide. She is the author of *Communication with All Life* and *Energy Healing for Animals*, and she's the founder of Communication with All Life University. Joan's work has been featured on the *Today* show, *Good Morning America*, and *Animal Planet*. For more, visit joanranquet.com.

Geneen Roth is a writer and teacher whose work focuses on using addiction as a path to the inner universe. She has written bestselling books and is a frequent guest on national radio and television shows, including *20/20* and *The Oprah Winfrey Show*. Geneen's most recent books are *Women Food and God: An Unexpected Path to Almost Everything* and *Women Food and God Coloring Book*. Information about her upcoming workshops is at geneenroth.com.

When not studying with Master Zephyr, **JP Sears** is an international teacher, speaker, and performer at events around the world. He's also an emotional-healing coach, curious student of life, and satirist who's best known for his popular YouTube-channel Ultra Spiritual videos, which have accumulated more than 100 million views. JP is also the author of a book, *How to Be Ultra Spiritual: 12½ Steps to Spiritual Superiority*. His website is awakenwithjp.com.

Mirabai Starr is a critically acclaimed author, translator, and speaker. Among the works she has translated are John of the Cross's *Dark Night of the Soul*, Teresa of Ávila's *The Book of My Life* and *The Interior Castle*, and *The Showings of Julian of Norwich*. She wrote reflections about the many aspects of Mary in *Mother of God Similar to Fire*. Mirabai's passionate exploration of the interconnected wisdom of the three Abrahamic faiths, *God of Love: A Guide to the Heart of Judaism* and *Christianity and Islam*, positions her at the forefront of the interspiritual movement. Her memoir, *Caravan of No Despair*, was listed in the "Best Spiritual Books of 2015" by the Spirituality & Practice website. Find out more at mirabaistarr.com.

Eckhart Tolle is the author of *The New York Times* bestseller *The Power of Now* (translated into thirty-three languages) and the highly acclaimed followup, *A New Earth*, which are widely regarded as two of the most influential spiritual books of our time. Eckhart is a sought-after public speaker and teaches and travels extensively throughout the world. Many of his talks, intensives, and retreats are published on CD and DVD. Most teachings are given in English, but occasionally Eckhart also gives talks in German and Spanish. Eckhart's book *Stillness Speaks* is designed for meditative reading, and *Practicing the Power of Now* consists of teachings, exercises, and meditations from *The Power of Now*. Immerse yourself in his teachings at eckharttolle.com.

Bonnie Myotai Treace Sensei is a Zen Teacher and writer who lives with her family in Garrison, New York, and Asheville, North Carolina. Her base is Gristmill Hermitage, in Hermitage Heart, in Garrison, where she leads meditation and writing retreats and does solitary work beside the millpond. She was the first dharma successor of John Daido Loori, founder of the Mountains and Rivers Order. Myotai's life as a Zen priest, feminist, poetry professor, and (somewhat obsessive) animal lover informs her writing. Myotai is the author of *Empty Branches* and *Winter Moon*, both in the Four Seasons of Zen Teachings series. She has contributed chapters to *Lotus Moon: The Poetry of Rengetsu*; *Water: Its Spiritual Significance*; *The Art of Just Sitting*; and *The Hidden Lamp: Stories from Twenty-Five Centuries of Awakened Women*. Visit 108bowls.org for more information.

A public figure, incarnate lama, teacher of Tibetan Buddhist philosophy, and published author of more than a dozen books, **His Eminence Tsem Tulku Rinpoche** is the founder of Tsem Rinpoche Foundation USA, Yayasan Kechara Indonesia, and Kechara Buddhist Association in Malaysia. He is an active proponent of vegetarianism, animal rescue, mind transformation, and compassion in action. Tsem Rinpoche inspires many to change their lives for the better and to practice kindness, tolerance, and integrity. He is beloved for his unconventional, contemporary approach to Buddhism and his unique ability to effortlessly bridge the East and the West, tirelessly sharing new ways and means of bringing happiness and relief to people from all walks of life through creative and engaging methods. Visit his website at tsemtulku.com.

Lama Tsomo—born Linda Pritzker—is an author, teacher, and ordained holder of the Namchak Buddhist lineage of Tibet. She's the cofounder of the Namchak Foundation and the author of two books, *The Princess Who Wept Pearls: The Feminine Journey in Fairytales* and *Why Is the Dalai Lama Always Smiling?: A Westerner's Introduction and Guide to Tibetan Buddhist Practice*. Learn more about Lama Tsomo and Namchak at namchak.org.

Alice Walker is an American novelist, short-story writer, poet, and activist. She wrote the critically acclaimed novel *The Color Purple*, for which she won the National Book Award and the Pulitzer Prize for Fiction. Her website is alicewalkersgarden.com.

Susanna Weiss is the executive director and a teacher at the Community Meditation Center in New York City. She has practiced meditation since 2000, studying with Sharon Salzberg, Thich Nhat Hanh, Allan Lokos, Andrew Olendzki, Tsoknyi Rinpoche, and others. She has taught at Columbia University Buddhist Association, New York Insight Meditation Center, Marymount Manhattan College, and The New Seminary. A former professional dancer, Susanna is also an ordained Interfaith minister. She is now in training as a Somatic Experiencing Practitioner.

Called "the most intriguing African-American Buddhist" by *Library Journal,* **Rev. angel Kyodo williams,** is an author, maverick spiritual teacher, master trainer, and founder of Center for Transformative Change. She has been bridging the worlds of personal transformation and justice since the publication of her critically acclaimed *Being Black: Zen and the Art of Living with Fearlessness and Grace*. Her book was hailed as "an act of love" by Pulitzer Prize winner Alice Walker and "a classic" by Buddhist teacher Jack Kornfield. Her most recent book, *Radical Dharma*, explores racial injustice as a barrier to collective awakening. For more, visit angelkyodowilliams.com.

About National Mill Dog Rescue

National Mill Dog Rescue's mission is to rescue, rehabilitate and rehome discarded breeding dogs and to educate the general public about the cruel realities of the commercial dog breeding industry. We are a 501(c)(3) non-profit organization located in Peyton, Colorado. To date we have rescued and rehomed more than 11,100 dogs. For more information please visit milldogrescue.org.

National Mill Dog Rescue™

About Sounds True

Sounds True is a multimedia publisher whose mission is to inspire and support personal transformation and spiritual awakening. Founded in 1985 and located in Boulder, Colorado, we work with many of the leading spiritual teachers, thinkers, healers, and visionary artists of our time. We strive with every title to preserve the essential "living wisdom" of the author or artist. It is our goal to create products that not only provide information to a reader or listener, but that also embody the quality of a wisdom transmission.

For those seeking genuine transformation, Sounds True is your trusted partner. At SoundsTrue.com you will find a wealth of free resources to support your journey, including exclusive weekly audio interviews, free downloads, interactive learning tools, and other special savings on all our titles.

To learn more, please visit SoundsTrue.com/freegifts or call us toll-free at 800.333.9185.

SOUNDS TRUE
many voices, one journey